GHOST TOWN STORIES II

GHOST TOWN STORIES II

From Renegade to Ruin Along the Red Coat Trail

HISTORY

by Johnnie Bachusky

For Darlis and Darlana

PUBLISHED BY ALTITUDE PUBLISHING CANADA LTD.
1500 Railway Avenue, Canmore, Alberta T1W 1P6
www.altitudepublishing.com
1-800-957-6888

Extreme care has been taken to ensure that all information presented in
this book is accurate and up to date. Neither the author nor the
publisher can be held responsible for any errors.

Publisher	Stephen Hutchings
Associate Publisher	Kara Turner
Editor	Georgina Montgomery

We acknowledge the financial support of the Government
of Canada through the Book Publishing Industry Development
Program (BPIDP) for our publishing activities.

Altitude GreenTree Program
Altitude Publishing will plant twice as many trees as were used
in the manufacturing of this product.

National Library of Canada Cataloguing in Publication Data

Bachusky, Johnnie
  Ghost towns stories II: from renegade to ruin along the Red Coat Trail
/ Johnnie Bachusky.

(Amazing stories)
Includes bibliographical references.
ISBN 1-55153-992-6

1. Ghost towns--Alberta--History. 2. Ghost towns--Saskatchewan--
History. 3. Alberta--History. 4. Saskatchewan--History. I. Title. II. Series:
Amazing stories (Canmore, Alta.)
FC3239.R43B32 2003   971.2   C2003-911122-9

An application for the trademark for Amazing Stories™
has been made and the registered trademark is pending.

Printed and bound in Canada by Friesens
4 6 8 9 7 5 3

Cover: The crumbling remains of Scotsguard's Lutheran Church in 2000.
Photograph by Johnnie Bachusky.

Contents

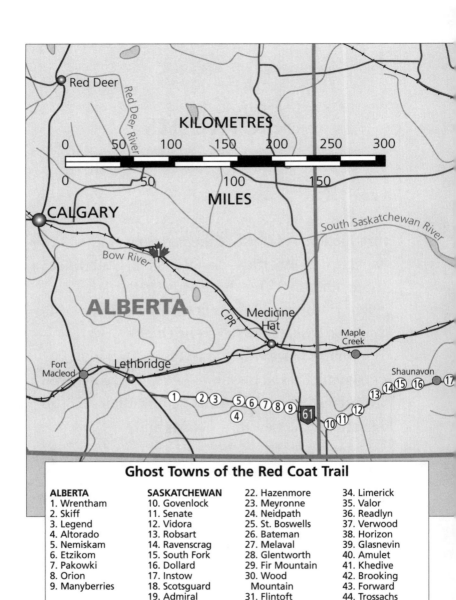

Ghost Towns of the Red Coat Trail

ALBERTA
1. Wrentham
2. Skiff
3. Legend
4. Altorado
5. Nemiskam
6. Etzikom
7. Pakowki
8. Orion
9. Manyberries

SASKATCHEWAN
10. Govenlock
11. Senate
12. Vidora
13. Robsart
14. Ravenscrag
15. South Fork
16. Dollard
17. Instow
18. Scotsguard
19. Admiral
20. Crichton
21. Gouverneur

22. Hazenmore
23. Meyronne
24. Neidpath
25. St. Boswells
26. Bateman
27. Melaval
28. Glentworth
29. Fir Mountain
30. Wood
    Mountain
31. Flintoft
32. Lakenheath
33. Stonehenge

34. Limerick
35. Valor
36. Readlyn
37. Verwood
38. Horizon
39. Glasnevin
40. Amulet
41. Khedive
42. Brooking
43. Forward
44. Trossachs

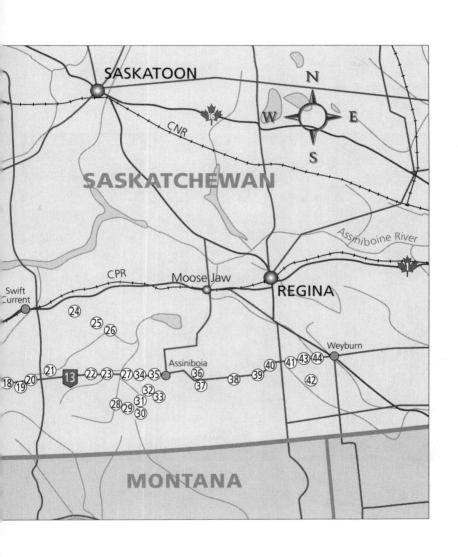

Ghost Town Stories II

Island's Hardware Store in Scotsguard in 2000.
(For the story turn to "Little Chicago" on page 66.)

Prologue

March 16, 1940. Arthur Barker has seen enough trouble over the past week. Farmers and ranchers throughout the Shaunavon district in Saskatchewan are going through hard times. Many people are still struggling from the Depression years and have barely enough to eat. Some of the communities in the district, known historically as the Red Coat Trail region, are already ghost towns. Now there have been reports of horse and cattle stealing. Arthur, an RCMP sergeant with special duties to investigate the thefts, is popular with local folks and concerned about what's been going on.

It's shortly after 9 p.m. and Arthur has just finished spending two turbulent hours with Victor Greenlay, a troubled man from the Climax district. Victor had called Arthur earlier in the evening and asked the officer to meet him in a room at the Grand Hotel. The meeting was bizarre. Victor, proclaiming he had found religion, prattled on like a lunatic. He wanted Arthur to help him prevent the federal government selling horses to France.

Victor believed horses would be Canada's only salvation. Arthur had listened patiently, but knew there was nothing he could do.

Finally, Arthur leaves. On his way downstairs to the lobby, he meets local Eileen Whittington. They exchange a few words before Arthur sits down at the bottom of the stairs to put on his boots.

He hears footsteps behind him. It's Victor, holding a .38 revolver. Three shots are fired.

In an upstairs room, J.J. Castle is startled by the blasts, thinking somebody has set off firecrackers. He heads down to the lobby, where he sees Victor standing over a fallen man at the bottom of the stairs. There's s blood all over the floor.

"Get back!" shouts Victor. "That's the devil lying there. He has to die!"

Introduction
Ghosts of the Red Coat Trail

G eoff Payne and I were eagerly up for the challenge. It was July 1995 and we were going on a ghost town expedition, something neither of us had done before. Geoff volunteered to be the driver. We were travelling to Alberta's Highway 61, located in the deep south of the province.

Geoff and I had never visited this area. We were intrigued that the highway had been, several years earlier, renamed the Red Coat Trail. The name change was in honour of the North West Mounted Police (NWMP), whose uniform coats were bright red. They made the famous 1874 March West through these southern regions of what is now Manitoba, Saskatchewan, and Alberta.

Geoff, a retired volunteer at Calgary's Kerby Centre (the nationally renowned senior citizens resource centre), was helping me with a feature story on ghost towns. He was well over 80 years old, but full of energy. He was moved by the degree of abandonment he saw at each community, as well as by the amazing stories we were told by remaining citizens.

This was a land of history, where Red Coats once saddled up and thundered across the plains during the era of 19th century Wild West living. For years, the Red Coats chased down bootleggers and safe-cracking gangsters across the southern plains of Manitoba to the foothills of Alberta and down to the American border. Big Muddy, for instance, was once an NWMP border post, built at the turn of the late 1900s to nab American rumrunners and outlaws, including Butch Cassidy and the Sundance Kid. Not long after the Red Coats arrived in 1874, the land became the hunting ground for famed Sioux leader Sitting Bull and his followers. They came to southern Saskatchewan soon after their 1876 victory over U.S. Calvary General George Custer at the Battle of Little Bighorn.

In the early years of the 20th century, frontier towns sprang up every 10 kilometres along rail lines.

They were home for thousands of settlers who travelled west to the Alberta foothills during the country's last great land rush. Many a hard-earned fortune was padded or lost in raucous hotels and pool halls, where high-stakes poker games went on all night. It was the duty of the Red Coats to maintain law and order in these new towns. Sometimes they paid for it with their lives.

When Geoff and I arrived at Orion, a community that resembles a classic ghost town from a Hollywood movie set, a group of elderly farmers were chatting over coffee in a hardware store. It was one of only two businesses still operating in the town (population, seven).

"The writing is on the wall," said Boyd Stevens, the store owner. He told us that Orion's last grain elevator — the town's final ray of hope — was about to be demolished. It was one of many slated to fall along the trail. There was once lots of hope, added one old-timer, but things never got any better.

The Red Coat Trail, while picturesque and historical, is a land of ghosts. In the face of the ravages of typhoid fever, drought, dust storms, rabbits, and grasshoppers, most hopes of prosperity gradually faded amongst the settlers. And any family homesteads remaining after all that were, for the most part, swallowed up by corporate grain farmers and ranchers. Once the people left, the communities dried up too.

What's left today are numerous ghost towns — what I define as former communities that are now shadows of their former selves. Not all ghost town are completely abandoned, but most are pretty close to empty, with perhaps just a handful of dedicated residents left.

As Geoff and I drove home that night after more than 16 hours on the road, I began to wonder about those who had gone before me on this mystical route. One whirlwind journey just didn't cut it. I had to go back. I wasn't sure when, but I knew I had some sort of future there, even if it meant just looking at the past.

Three years after my trip, Calgarian Don Sucha, accompanied by his two children, paid a visit of his own to the Red Coat Trail. Their journey took them to southern Saskatchewan where the trail, now Highway 13, is linked to Alberta's historic roadway.

In 1997, Don had discovered the gravesite of NWMP Constable Daniel "Peach" Davis in Calgary while visiting the city's Union Cemetery. Peach was Don's great grand-uncle and an NWMP Red Coat who served at the Wood Mountain post in the late 1870s and early 1880s.

As a child, Don had heard stories from relatives about Peach, who was dubbed a folk hero for his extraordinary single-handed escort of hundreds of displaced Native peoples in 1882.

As a grade school student in the 1950s, Don read stories about Peach and heard about him during lessons. But he had little interest in learning more — until that day he found Peach's grave. Then he was hooked. He knew he had to go back along the Red Coat Trail to Wood Mountain.

A few hours after entering Saskatchewan, Don drove south from the Trans-Canada Highway to Highway 13. Almost immediately, they began passing one ghost town after another. They wouldn't have noticed some: those had simply vanished. Others, such as Robsart, Dollard, and Scotsguard, have a few inhabitants but no services. They contain rows of empty and boarded-up homes and businesses.

Don and his children decided to stay the night at the Wood Mountain campground.

They arrived in the town a few days after the area's well-known stampede had finished for another year. First held in 1890, the Wood Mountain Stampede is the oldest continuously running rodeo in Canada. It attracts up to 5000 people. When Don turned up, however, both the campground and the village were empty and desolate, filled only by the intermittent howling of the wind.

"The campground looked like a scene out of the film *The Grapes of Wrath*," remembers Don, a Calgary museum technician. "And going into town was like entering a ghost town."

Wood Mountain's last businesses, a hotel and café, had shut down several years earlier. The school closed in 1994. One old grain elevator still stands, but it's rarely open to visitors. The village's only remaining enterprises are its municipal office and a rural post office.

Mayor Michael Klein has no problem with anyone calling his village a ghost town. "The townsite has shrunk as small as it can shrink," he says.

The Wood Mountain community first took root in 1911 as a service centre for ranching homesteaders. The townsite was moved eight kilometres north in 1928 alongside the rail line. It quickly prospered, reaching a peak population of about 250 people. But, like so many towns and villages in the region, it declined during the Depression years and never recovered.

The original NWMP post here was first used by a British North America Boundary Commission survey team in the early 1870s to map out a boundary line between Canada and the United States. The post was taken over by a detachment of NWMP officers in 1874, who made the historic 1300-kilometre March West trek across the western Canadian frontier.

"The Mounties would never have made it west had it not been for a Boundary Commission depot with food and supplies at Wood Mountain," says Thelma Poirier, a regional historian who has lived all her life near Wood Mountain. "They intended to live off the land, but they were totally unaware that hardly anything was out there for them to live off."

The original detachment of more than 200 Red Coats was sent by Ottawa to establish law and order. Whiskey traders were out of control — and so, too, wolfers, who had been responsible for the Cypress Hills Massacre the year before. Ottawa also wanted peaceful negotiations initiated with the west's Native peoples.

Along the way, the Red Coats erected posts at Fort Saskatchewan, Fort Calgary, Fort Macleod, and Fort Walsh, the latter named for its commanding officer, Superintendent James Walsh. It was Walsh who was sent by officials to meet Sitting Bull in 1876 after he fled the U.S. Sitting Bull respected Walsh and a peaceful agreement was reached. Walsh formed a new Wood Mountain detachment shortly after the deal. Sitting Bull made a promise — which he kept until returning to the U.S. years later — that the Sioux would respect Canadian laws.

Peach served with B Division at Fort Walsh, which also was responsible for the Wood Mountain post. In 1882, he received an assignment that would make him a Red Coat legend.

Government and police forces were trying to convince Native peoples from the prairie to put an end to the constant conflicts between rival groups on both sides of the borders. Part of the animosity was caused by bands crossing the border into the U.S. to hunt dwindling buffalo herds. American forces pushed them back to the border and asked Canadian authorities to take responsibility. However, there was a manpower shortage within NWMP ranks, created by the extensive duties of watching over Sitting Bull and his warriors.

But Peach was available. He was the lone Red Coat sent to the American border to escort up to 300 Assiniboine almost 250 kilometres to Battleford, Saskatchewan, where they were to be dispersed on existing reserves.

When the 23-year-old Peach met the Assiniboine for the long journey, he discovered they had accepted their fate gracefully. The group travelled slowly, making only 16 kilometres a day. During the entire trip, Peach was mindful of the ongoing conflict between the Assiniboine and the Blackfoot. The first sign of trouble occurred at Fort Walsh when Peach and his group replenished supplies. The Blackfoot made a show of force nearby. Next morning, one of the Assiniboine was found dead. During the journey, Peach and his group also had to contend with a large number of horse and supply thefts.

When Peach and the Assiniboine reached

Battleford after three weeks, he was rewarded with a new uniform — that and the new name he received from the Assiniboine, "Got-Mad-All-The-Time."

Peach went on to serve in the North West Rebellion in 1885 and was discharged from the force in 1886. His life after the NWMP was often difficult and trying. He died in poverty in March 1937 at Calgary's Holy Cross Hospital. He was 83 years old.

The story of the lone Mountie escorting hundreds of Assiniboine was a popular RCMP tale for much of the first half of the 20th century. However, the authenticity of Peach's story has since been challenged by the RCMP. Historians with the force say Peach's tale became entangled with another incident at the Alberta border in 1896.

The only way Don was going to learn more was to find out himself by visiting Wood Mountain and other Red Coat Trail locales where Peach served.

"I started my research, thinking that this story was an exaggeration by an old man telling tales," says Don. "The further I got into it, I discovered there was more truth in the story than fiction."

Don's quest would not be an easy task. Peach was not famous like James Walsh or Sitting Bull. Historical records of Peach's 1882 achievement are often sketchy and contradictory. But Don's trip in 1998 was a start in the right place. Wood Mountain is the heart of the Red

Coat Trail. Some say the land still hums, breathes, and even aches from the trials and celebrations of days long past.

Those Red Coat Trail spirits have called me back many times since 1995. When my wife Darlis and I got married in 2001, we took a camping trip along the Red Coat Trail on our honeymoon. We stopped and stayed the night at Wood Mountain. The wind was calm that evening. The distant voices of the past were just waiting to speak. Now, in this book, they finally can.

Manyberries, Alberta
Gangsters and Outlaws

L yle Nattress was an original Manyberries newspaper hawker. For many years in the 1920s, the diminutive Lyle was a familiar and entertaining fixture in town. Several nights and mornings a week, he could be heard on street corners, inside liquor joints, and even on incoming trains yelling, "Extra, extra! Read all about it!"

When the railway arrived in 1916, Manyberries became a booming pioneer town, growing to more than 200 citizens by 1921 and serving a trading area of more than 1000 farmers and ranchers. With the constant arrival of settlers, delivery of the news was not only in demand in Manyberries, it was generated locally on a daily basis. These were the Roaring Twenties — the prohibition years — and bootleggers, rum-runners, and outlaws dominated the headlines. They were hot news, and Lyle's hawking got everybody's attention.

Each train night, Lyle received 30 copies of the *Lethbridge Herald* and 10 of the *Calgary Herald*. He paid two cents a paper and sold them for five cents. For a kid, it was hard work with long hours, especially in winter when trains, which were supposed to arrive at 6 p.m., were frequently late. His job, however, was to sell papers, and even if Lyle had to wait as long as four hours, he not only stayed at the station to gather up his bundles, he boarded the train and hawked his papers to the passengers. Once finished there, he hit the pool rooms and bars.

"There wasn't any law against a newsboy going into the pool rooms in those days," Lyle recounted in an interview in 1985. "They were nearly always filled with players or spectators sitting on the benches so it was an excellent place to sell papers. In the early 1920s, before the town's hotel had a beer parlour, hard liquor was sold over the counter in the Nowak Billiard Hall, and I often received tips from the patrons. I guess Manyberries was a little wild in those days."

Lyle was not only a messenger of the news from the

The former Manyberries train station photographed in 2000. The train station had long been closed and the rail tracks pulled.

world outside Manyberries, he was privy to most of the good yarns right in town. While on hawking rounds from one business to another along Main Street, he invariably encountered a few of the characters in the small town on the Red Coat Trail. One of these was Nels Draege, operator of a pool hall and the town barber. Nels was famous for his sense of humour and penchant for drinking binges.

However, according to Lyle, it seemed that no matter how much he drank, Nels could still shave a man without making a nick.

The likeable barber always had a caper up his sleeve. One of his chairs was wired to a six-volt battery, which Nels could switch on with his foot while he cut someone's hair. When a new or unsuspecting customer came in for a cut, Nels slyly waited for his opportunity. "The victim usually let out a yell and jumped into the air, much to the amusement of all those present," remembered Lyle.

There would be a thousand more local stories Lyle would collect in his hawking days, many of them recounted in a Manyberries community history book more than six decades later.

Lyle's boyhood newspaper days included the delivery of some of the most sensational and bizarre news events ever to strike the communities along the Red Coat Trail. Every year, as the railways began to stretch their lines west, pioneer communities along the Red Coat Trail from Manitoba to Alberta were considered easy targets for bandits and outlaws. Some of the more notorious gangs operated out of Havre, Montana, and Minot, North Dakota. The gangsters knew full well that the new frontier north of the border had several isolated farming communities protected only with marginal law enforcement resources. More often than not, the burden of law enforcement fell to the North West Mounted

Police or to the provincial police forces of the three provinces.

In those pioneer days, the provinces had only one policeman per 1600 square kilometres of settlement. By the 1920s, American bandits were so brazen along the Red Coat Trail, they were hitting banks in broad daylight. In September 1922, armed robbers from south of the border struck banks on two consecutive nights in Moosemin and Ceylon in Saskatchewan, pulling off a sensational early morning caper in the latter's Bank of Montreal by cutting off telephone and telegraph lines and blowing off bank and safe doors with nitroglycerine. The bandits headed south with more than $16,000 of the Ceylon bank's money and bonds. For many days after, the back-to-back Saskatchewan robberies were front-page news across the west, including in the papers in Lyle's bundles. However, these paled in comparison to the heist a month earlier in Foremost, 67 kilometres west of Manyberries along Alberta's Red Coat Trail.

On August 29, a group of outlaws from a Havre gang were putting the final touches to a grand scheme to rob Foremost's Union Bank. It was the same gang that had pulled off robberies in the border towns of Ladner, British Columbia, and Mathers, Manitoba, as well as in Dollard, Saskatchewan, along the Red Coat Trail. They had come three days earlier to scout and plan their heist, which was later considered the most daring ever staged in the history of southern Alberta.

Although these men were criminals, they were cunning enough to blend and socialize with unsuspecting locals, despite weeks of public warnings to Foremost citizens from police that a gang of professional American bank thieves was operating in border towns. A few hours before the robbery, the outlaws broke into the Canadian Pacific Railway warehouse and stole a heavy hammer and crow bar. They also cut all the telegram and telephone wires, breaking Foremost's connection to the outside world. In the early morning hours, a junior clerk by the name of Jennings, who was asleep in the guard room at the rear of the bank, was awakened by beams of a flashlight shining on him and a colleague through a window.

"An automatic revolver of seemingly gigantic proportions was playing on me," Jennings later told authorities. "One man said, 'Be quiet, we won't hurt you. We're just going to hold up the bank.'"

The gang forced Jennings to open the vault, but they still had to blow up an inner door with a charge of nitroglycerine. They made off with tens of thousands of dollars in cash and non-negotiable victory bonds and securities. The outlaws had planned their job well, tying up the bank clerks, removing parts of automobiles parked in the street, and placing large rocks on the roads near the bank to prevent an immediate police pursuit. Their getaway car was hidden in a haystack on the edge of town. They made the border, but their time on the lam was soon over. They were caught in the U.S. and sentenced to lengthy prison terms. The investigation by the Alberta Provincial Police made international headlines, as it ultimately broke up what was then considered to be North America's most sophisticated bank robbery ring.

Manyberries was not immune to bandits either, but as everybody soon learned after the town's most noteworthy robbery in 1916, the deed was not sophisticated like that of Havre's gang. Still, it made a great newspaper yarn. At the very least, the Manyberries heist had good planning leading to the stick-up. The bandits deliberately picked a town that sat close to the border, had minimal police resources, and lacked telephone and telegraph services.

While other well-documented pioneer Red Coat Trail robberies took weeks and even months to crack by police, the Manyberries robbery of 1916 was a hair-raising affair that lasted only 20 minutes. It also made headlines across western Canada, although it occurred too early for Lyle's newspaper delivering days. The caper began in the morning of December 2, 1916, when two

New York City men, Alexander McLaughlin and James Wilson, approached William Huggins at a public auto stand in Medicine Hat. They told Huggins they were cattle buyers and needed to be chauffeured to Manyberries, about 70 kilometres south of Medicine Hat. After paying Huggins $25 in advance, the trio reached Manyberries around noon. The New Yorkers had a brief lunch at George Holdershaw's hotel and then told Huggins they were heading to the local Canadian Bank of Commerce branch to make a transaction.

The bank was closed for lunch, but the bank manager, T.C. MacDonald, let them in after being told by the pair they needed to make a small deposit. MacDonald was preparing a deposit slip when he heard, "Hands up!" A glance showed him that a Colt .45 revolver was aimed at his assistant, D.E. Withington, and the barrel of another gun was sighted on his own head.

By this time, McLaughlin and Wilson had pulled neckerchiefs up over the lower portion of their faces. They then bound and gagged the bank employees before helping themselves to more than $15,000 in cash that was lying in an open box in Withington's desk. Before making their getaway, the two men told the bank employees not to sound the alarm for at least an hour or an accomplice outside would storm in and knock them over the heads.

The employees — unaware there was no accomplice outside — were also told by the thieves that this was not a robbery: it was only a loan to cover their margins from a huge wheat market loss. They were also told the loan would be returned in a couple of months.

The men fled the bank and raced back to the hotel where Huggins, unaware that a robbery had taken place, was waiting. The two barked at him, "Get us away quick!" Before their now-suspicious chauffeur could ask questions, they tossed him a $10 tip for his efforts. Huggins told them his car needed oil first, and he drove it a kilometre and a half towards a garage just outside town.

Meanwhile, back at the bank, the employees were working on the knots in their ropes and gags. Fortuitously, local customer Charlie Burr knocked on the door, wanting to do some banking. "We called to him that the bank had been robbed and that we were tied up and asked him to break in the window," MacDonald later told Mounties. "Burr gave the alarm and a couple of men arrived and cut our bonds."

A posse, which included MacDonald, quickly jumped into a car and raced in the direction the bandits were last seen heading. It didn't take them long to spot the men at the garage where Huggins was now cranking the auto while Wilson stood in the car and McLaughlin paced. As the posse wheeled in at top speed, Wilson immediately threw up his hands. At the same time, posse member Vern McLean took a leap from the chase vehicle's running board and landed on Huggins, roughing him up without realizing he was an innocent party.

"I fired two shots from my revolver, one at the tall man [McLaughlin], who disappeared within the garage, and one at the other man [Wilson] who threw up his hands and surrendered," said MacDonald.

The stolen money was seized and Wilson was bound and taken back to town. More armed men arrived and circled the garage where McLaughlin was hiding. After a few warning shots were fired, he finally surrendered. The entire drama was over in 20 minutes. McLaughlin and Wilson were taken back to Manyberries. A blacksmith cut a length of chain into shackles and these were secured on the prisoners with six padlocks. The two were taken to Medicine Hat that night and brought before court the following morning.

Although Lyle was too young to hawk the news of the famous 1916 bank robbery to his fellow citizens, he was close to a hair-raising family experience a decade later. It was another one of those Red Coat Trail adventures that included guns, booze, and desperate outlaws.

In July 1926, his family embarked on a four-month covered wagon trip to a farm 60 kilometres east of

Prince Albert, Saskatchewan. They were delivering 80 head of horses. A few days after they left, one of the horses ran off into heavy brush alongside the Red River at Blindloss, Alberta. Lyle's father and two helpers gave chase, but 16 kilometres up the river, they encountered trouble.

"They ran into a still where a man was making whiskey," recounted Lyle several years later. "He threatened to shoot them, but after they persuaded him they were only looking for a horse and he could go on making all the whiskey he wanted to, he let them go."

Lyle's dad and the helpers caught the horse and brought it back to camp. The men decided to take a bath in the river. Almost immediately, there was more trouble. "No sooner had they got into the water than shells started to drop around them," said Lyle. "We quickly moved camp, as we didn't think this was a very healthy place to stay."

Lyle's newspaper days in Manyberries eventually came to an end and he became a school teacher and a rancher. Although he sold his ranch in 1979 and moved to Lethbridge to retire (where he died in 1996), he was already instrumental during the 1970s in having Highway 61 in Alberta renamed the Red Coat Trail.

At the same time, Lyle, a county councillor, was a key figure in persuading the Alberta government to extend the southern Alberta roadway from Manyberries to the Saskatchewan border, linking it to Highway 13 in that province. In 1981, RCMP officials in Ottawa renamed Highway 61 in Alberta, and the linking highways in Saskatchewan and Manitoba, the Red Coat Trail. Road markers, depicting a Mountie in an 1874 uniform, were placed along the tri-province highway system from Winnipeg to Fort Macleod, indicating the points where the modern roadway crossed the historic North West Mounted Police route.

This time Lyle not only delivered the news to grateful folks in Manyberries and others along the Red Coat Trail, he was a deserving headline himself.

Orion, Alberta

The Mysterious Dr. Bartlett

There were two certainties about Dr. Samuel Bartlett. He never turned down a good country home-cooked meal, and he never ever told anyone why he left Boston and its prestigious medical community to live in the untamed western Canadian frontier.

"He took that secret to his grave," says Boyd Stevens, who in 2003 is one of only six remaining citizens in the Red Coat Trail hamlet of Orion.

There was no mystery, however, behind "Doc's" appetite. It was legendary throughout southeastern Alberta. And so was Doc's lifestyle, one of poverty and squalor. Still, he was loved and respected by all, even if he was usually unkempt and unwashed.

He never asked for payment for medical services, and he would stay and sit with sick or injured patients, especially children, for days at a time. But he'd happily take advantage of any free dining offers. In fact, the good doctor, whose kindness and generosity moved locals in the Glassford district for more than four decades, designed a perfect system to ensure he never went hungry during his travels.

"When he was living in the little dugout by Manyberries Creek, he used to walk the grub line," remembers Kay Dann, who was treated by Doc when growing up near Orion. "He would go to one person's for suppertime, and then the next day he would hit the next person's place. He was pretty ingenious when it came to surviving."

It was quite the turnaround from fancy Boston living where the permanent bachelor had the best of everything: status, high society friends, and wealth. In Orion, he adopted a dramatically different lifestyle — an impoverished, solitary existence in a one-room dugout shack on Manyberries Creek, about 10 kilometres southwest of the town. The shack was situated on a small acreage, over-populated with pigs, horses, and cats. Everyone knew Doc loved animals, but once in a while when visiting his quarters, guests had to contend with new wildlife surprises. One story tells of a former patient declining Doc's offer of a cup of coffee after spotting a muskrat swimming in a shack pail. According to another tale, someone once saw garter snakes slithering through the shelves of Doc's medicine cabinet.

"Once he was having something to eat and there were some mice running across the table," says Boyd. "He just shooed them off like he would've done to a fly. I guess it just didn't bother him."

Cats held a special place in Doc's heart. There was always a clowder of felines lodging with him in his 8-foot by 10-foot squatter's shack, jumping around on his eating table or doing whatever they pleased. The loyal felines had to compete for space in the tiny cabin with hundreds of magazines and medical journals. Doc may not have prided himself on housekeeping, but he was a voracious reader and loved to argue with locals, especially Kay's father, Sydney, about politics and economics.

The pigs, thankfully for visitors, ran wild outside, multiplying and creating havoc. "Of course his neighbours were kind of peeved at times," recalled Boyd's father, Howard, before he passed away in 1990. "But being old Doc, he got away with it."

Doc was born in Boston, New England on April 25, 1875. It is known that his father, George Pinksham

Bartlett, attended Harvard Medical School from 1869 to 1871, studying both dentistry and medicine. He became a widely respected surgeon in the Boston area. The younger Bartlett graduated from the same school in 1899 and joined his father's medical practice. Sometime during his schooling, Doc lost the sight in one eye, the result of an ice hockey injury. It's also known that Bartlett Senior passed away suddenly of meningitis a year after Doc's graduation. In later years, Doc would speak to locals about his former way of life in Boston, but never offered an explanation as to why he left and would never return.

"My husband's father sometimes used to go to Havre, Montana, and he would ask Doc to come along, but Doc would never cross that border," says Kay. "We supposed he was a wanted man or something. He never talked about it to any of us."

The details of Doc's life between his father's death and when he first set up a homestead on the bank of Manyberries Creek in 1911 are even more sketchy. It was certainly a time when tens of thousands of people, many of them immigrants from the U.S., were enticed to the western prairie frontier on the Canadian federal government's offer of plentiful free land. Whether this was at least part of Doc's motive to leave New England has never been confirmed, but it is known that he drifted throughout western Canada before settling near Orion.

Doc worked as a field pitcher in 1910 on a threshing crew in Manitoba, and then briefly held a job as a construction worker at Fort Steele, British Columbia. Later he worked as a labourer on the Lethbridge Irrigation Project.

After Doc settled at Manyberries Creek, and later in Orion itself, there were rumours and whispered speculation over what had happened in Doc's life.

"People had different ideas," says Kay's older sister, Margaret, who was also a recipient of Doc's medical services as a youth. "Some people thought it was drink. My mother always felt that he had performed an abortion on somebody and they squealed on him in Boston. We just didn't know."

For anyone looking at Orion today, it's hard to imagine that this dying community of half a dozen people held so much attraction, promise, and hope for hundreds during the initial wave of settlers in the early 20th century. Today it's a ghost-towner's dream, with a score of empty and abandoned buildings, some of them dating back to when Doc himself was walking the grub line. The Stevens even hauled a Canadian Pacific Railway section house from Pakowki, 11 kilometres west, and moved it into town. Pakowki is one of the many communities along Alberta's Red Coat Trail that vanished decades ago. Many locals fear the same fate for Orion.

Ironically, it was Pakowki's pending doom that helped contribute to Orion's early promise. By about 1915, settlers in Pakowki became disillusioned with the hardships of pioneer life and the rocky and barren land that proved unproductive for farming. When the railway pushed farther east, many residents and their businesses followed. Orion was then officially put on the map in 1916, a group of citizens naming the new town after the constellation. Orion grew quickly, and by 1922 had more than 30 businesses, including a bank, a hotel, and four grain elevators. The future looked bright, but a prolonged drought through most of the 1920s initiated a decline from which the town could never recover. By the latter part of the decade, many homesteaders were bankrupt and gladly accepted the Alberta government's offers of free transportation to move to other parts of the province.

Doc, meanwhile, chose to stay. He appeared pleased with his simple life, earning a few dollars here and there by growing cereal crops and watermelons. Doc's farming skills, however, were negligible. He had no money for proper machinery and lacked improvisational know-how to make ends meet. He ultimately went bankrupt as well and lost his homestead. Fortunately, his land was bought up by a kind neighbour who let Doc keep his dugout and livestock. Such generosity reflected not only the fact that Doc was well liked, but that he was so appreciated for the immense contribution he had made to the community.

When the worldwide flu epidemic swept the region in 1918 and 1919, Doc became the area's medical health officer and was granted a special permit by the provincial government to practise medicine. Following the outbreak, he was offered a position at Medicine Hat's Medical Arts Clinic — a position he refused.

Although some locals could afford to pay Doc for his services, he still never asked for money. A meal or some produce to take home, yes; and he was partial to a nice snag of snuff, or "snooze" as locals called it. Local men were known to carry two boxes of snuff, one for themselves and another for Doc. When the always-broke Doc was offered a pinch of snooze, he'd snatch it with his special three-finger-and-one-thumb grip, which became known as the "three-fingered snooze alger."

"Money didn't mean anything to him," recalls Kay. "When his shack burned down once, my husband was up there fighting the fire. He said he found three or four old-age pension cheques about that Doc had never even cashed."

At the same time, Doc was always available for a call, even if it meant walking all day on dusty trails to treat the sick, deliver babies, or mend a broken arm. One time he trekked 80 kilometres to Medicine Hat during the scarlet fever epidemic in the late 1930s to bring back medicine for stricken Orion children.

"One time during a blizzard in either 1936 or 1937, he trudged through the snow to our house because I was so sick with the measles," recalls Kay, pausing. "It was doing that kind of thing that made him so important to everyone in the community."

On another occasion, Boyd came down with a stomach ache and Doc was brought to the house. Doc diagnosed appendicitis and even accompanied the Stevens family to Medicine Hat.

Doc had a special relationship with children. He adored them, even though many claimed they were spooked by the tall, bearded old country doctor. "We were scared of him, but I'm not sure why. He never hurt anybody," says Boyd. "I think it was because he had these scruffy whiskers. Back in those days, nobody wore whiskers."

Doc didn't gave notice he was ever offended by any overactive child's imagination. Instead, he always had candies for the children and was known to sit with sick kids for hours on end, playing cards and helping with their homework.

"I took my Grade 9 by correspondence and he

helped me with my geometry. I don't think I would have ever passed it without him," says Margaret. "He would work for hours and hours, and he would get the answer and then he would tell me how he got it, and then I could put it down the way it was supposed to be put down."

No one knew if Doc had ever married. He was never known to be hitched up with a woman in Canada, and folks never asked if there had been a special lady from his Boston days. Nevertheless, in the Orion area, Doc played the part of swinging bachelor at country dances. He loved to dance with the ladies, especially young school teachers. On these social occasions, he made it a point to look like the distinguished Boston doctor he may once have been. He would dress in a grey suit, with a clean shirt and tie on, and he would carry his dancing shoes to the hall, lest they got dusty during the long hike there. He was especially fond of a fast waltz, though — unfortunately for his partners — it made him perspire heavily.

"He would always pick on the young girls for a dance," says Margaret. "We used to try to hide because our parents told us we were never to turn him down."

As the years wore on, Doc's health began to deteriorate and he depended more and more on the love and support of locals. In 1953, his Orion home caught fire and he was seriously burned. He had to be hospitalized for several months in Medicine Hat. It was said at the time that Doc could have avoided serious injury from the fire if he hadn't tried to rescue a litter of kittens from under his bed.

When Doc was able to go back to his beloved Orion, residents had a new home built for him, complete with a garden. The community returned all the countless favours this mysterious gentleman had given them over the years, and made sure Doc was comfortable during his recovery.

On November 10, 1956, Doc passed away. His death was mourned from the Red Coat Trail region to Medicine Hat, where Doc was buried. The Medical Association of Medicine Hat had a special commemorative granite marker made and it was placed on Doc's grave at Hillside Cemetery.

Etzikom, Alberta
Winds of Change

When the wind blows through the Red Coat Trail community of Etzikom, it's considered a mixed blessing. On the one hand, according to Native folklore if the wind is a Chinook, it will bring the promise of warmth and hope. Native legend tells the story of a beautiful maiden named Chinook who was lost in the southwest mountains when she wandered away from her tribe. The bravest warriors spent several days searching for the lost maiden and were close to abandoning hope when a soft, warm wind blew in from the west. The warriors looked at each other in wonder.

"It is the spirit of our beautiful Chinook," said one warrior joyously.

Forever after, the warm southwest wind became known to Native peoples as the Chinook, bringing happiness through the comforting spirit of the lost maiden.

However, there's another type of Chinook that blows through Etzikom. Called the Manyberries Chinook, it is cold and menacing. While the town also experiences the better-known warm Chinooks originating from the Pacific, residents also brace for the Manyberries Chinook from the southeast. It originates in Saskatchewan, but has no means to warm up. As it blows over huge expanses of snow-blanketed fields and through Etzikom, the Manyberries Chinook increases the wintry frostiness covering the land. Since the turn of the century, residents have known the Manyberries Chinook to underscore harsh winters of bitter cold, deep snow, and vicious biting gales.

"The Pacific-born Chinook is a mixed blessing because it will melt the snow, but suck the moisture out of the ground in the summer. It's a dry wind," says long-time Etzikom resident Len Mitzel. "The Manyberries Chinook, on the other hand, is a cold wind."

Len is keenly aware of the wind's importance and place in his region's history. He is the curator of the Etzikom Museum of Southeast Alberta, which also includes the Canadian National Historic Windpower Centre, the first facility of its kind in North America.

"I remember when we first got electricity in the '50s. It was phenomenal when you could just flick a switch," says Len. "That was the sort of thing that water and a windmill did. Many of the farms on the prairies had a windmill."

But when the wind gave, it also took away. The early pioneer years of Etzikom and the area were noted for wind-driven calamities — blizzards and dust storms that created incredible hardship and despair for settlers.

* * *

Etzikom is a Blackfoot term meaning valley or coulee. The townsite was staked by the Canadian Pacific Railway in 1914. It was another new community along the rail line that pushed east, arriving in Etzikom in 1915. The new line was built through the labour of German and Austrian prisoners from World War I, with communities constructed every 12 to 16 kilometres. Etzikom lay between Pakowki in the east and Nemiskam in the west.

Even before 1915, the Etzikom area was witnessing a steady inflow of settlers who came from eastern Canada and the U.S. to take up the government's offer of free land and the promise of a better way of life. The

Main Street in Etzikom in 1917. The town was at the height of its
pioneer prosperity, which would be short-lived due to droughts.

construction of the railway gave the settlers added hope
their dreams would be fully realized.

"Those settlers took up homesteads in the 1908—
1910 land rush and lived desperately in sod shacks. They
wanted to improve their way of life, and as the railway
came through, it brought stock cars full of lumber," says
Len, whose family roots in the Etzikom area go back to
1908. "There were five lumberyards at one time," adds
Len. "As fast as they could get it off the cars and into the
lumberyards, people were coming with their wagons
and hauling it to their farms to build houses and barns."

There was a building frenzy in the fledgling town,
and a bit of controversy. A post official decided that

Etzikom was not a suitable name and changed it to Endon. This angered CPR officials, who changed it back to Etzikom in 1916.

District farmers all around the new town converted vast cattle lands to agriculture, and grain growers soon enjoyed memorable wheat harvests.

Etzikom's initial prosperity caught the attention of the *Lethbridge Herald*, which printed glowing articles on the new town. "For a town four weeks old, this place has surely had a phenomenal growth," reported the newspaper.

However, the hazards of living in a dry belt soon left a nasty mark on the town.

A fire broke out on April 14, 1916, in a department store. The blaze took a store safe with $3000 cash inside, municipal records, a billiard room, and a concert hall that was still under construction. Total damage exceeded $25,000 and there was no insurance.

While the town struggled to recover from the fire, the entire area was hit by the Spanish influenza in 1918, a worldwide epidemic that claimed 3300 Albertans that winter, including a score of Etzikom area residents. A temporary hospital was set up at the hotel and residents wore masks when they left their homes (as dictated by a provincial law passed on October 25, 1918).

"I can remember my dad saying that two or three of

the townspeople had hitched up wagons and travelled through the countryside to take bodies to the local mortuary that had been set up," says Charles Beer, whose parents moved to Etzikom in 1915 and opened a hardware store.

Following World War I, more bad times came, the result of years of drought, dust storms, and other natural disasters. Residents of Etzikom, which had seen a peak population of 300 during its brief time of prosperity, left in droves. Some were so destitute, they gave up their children for adoption, believing that just about anybody could give their young ones a better life than they could.

This plight of farmers and ranchers was documented by Charles's father in a letter to his brother in 1919:

"The situation is becoming rather serious in this area. They just shipped out in one week 3000 head of cattle. There are serious drought conditions…. There is no feed available, and no feed forthcoming from the government has been promised. The farmers are very upset."

In another letter written by Charles's mother on January 13, 1922, she told relatives that businesses in town were failing, the land was dried up, and the family was ready to leave as soon as they could get out of debt.

"I remember my mother mentioning that they had to go down to the station to meet the train because water was being delivered there in barrels," says Charles. "People took it back to their homes by the barrel. The farmers all around the town, helped by the townspeople, were hoping at that time to find some artesian wells."

But few were found, and the Beer family left Etzikom in 1925 to go to Olds, where they opened a new hardware store.

Two years after Charles and his family left, the town was hit by another disastrous fire, this one sweeping through the business district and destroying several buildings. Still, the town trudged on. From 1930 to 1970, the population fluctuated between 119 and 130. Those who chose to stay made the best of it, determined to persevere no matter what obstacle came their way. One of those hardy souls was Alfred Nielson, a Danish bachelor who believed in the old pioneer adage of "all work and no play." Locals say he was about as tough a cowboy as ever was made in the Canadian west.

"He had money, but he wouldn't spend it," remembers local rancher Ed Lee, who was born in the region in 1919 and still living on his farm in 2003. "He worked on the railroad in Minnesota and then came up here and homesteaded. He farmed a little bit, but mostly he raised cattle," says Ed. "He believed in the survival of the fittest. I don't think he enjoyed life that much; he spent all his time trying to make a living."

For many years, Alfred did not believe in dehorning his cattle because he thought they would lose too much weight. One morning, while he was attempting to load some two-year-old steers at the Etzikom stockyard, one broke away and ran past him. Suddenly the steer changed its mind and turned, its horn catching Alfred in the eye and popping it right out. According to Ed, Alfred walked almost a kilometre up to the filling station, holding his hand over his eye. He wanted the men there just to bandage him up so he could get back to work. The horrified garage workers convinced the cowboy to go to the hospital. Alfred spent the rest of his life with one eye, never bothering to obtain a cosmetic substitute.

The eye mangling was not Alfred's only accident. One afternoon, he was riding far out on his ranch when something caused his horse to rear. Alfred lost his seat and the horse fell on him, breaking his pelvis. After crawling all day and night, covering a distance of at least four kilometres, Alfred managed to climb to the top of a hill. That morning, a neighbouring rancher spotted Alfred up there and took the injured man to hospital.

"Everybody said Alfred would never ride again," recalls Ed. "But in less than a year he was back on a horse. He was a tough old geezer."

Alfred left the farm and went to Vancouver in the 1960s to retire and enjoy all the money he had hoarded during his life in Etzikom. He invested his money wisely and bought property. The local who had purchased Alfred's Etzikom-area property later went to visit the retired Danish cowboy, hoping all the man's hard work had finally given him a comfortable retirement.

"Turns out, however, that Alfred had met a woman there. Her son was a lawyer. I guess they somehow got most of his money," says Ed. "In the end, he never even had enough money to buy a newspaper."

In the mid-1980s, with the town's population dropping to fewer than 60 citizens, Etzikom suffered another blow. The school was closed, a victim of dwindling enrollment. As a viable community, it appeared Etzikom's days were numbered. The ghosts were knocking at the doors.

After almost two years of sitting vacant and being briefly owned by the Etzikom Recreation Club, the school was purchased by local history buffs Len and June Mitzel. In 1988, a non-profit museum society was formed with the goal of turning the old school into a regional public museum. The Mitzels transferred ownership of the building to the society.

Len and June completely renovated the three-classroom cinderblock building. Then, before the couple and museum volunteers could realize their dream of opening the facility in 1990, the project took a dramatic new direction. Etzikom native Bill Peters, who was living in Calgary at the time, came to town in 1988 to offer his assistance on a local history book project. He also seized the opportunity to give the society a presentation on his lifelong passion — windmills.

"Bill had travelled all over the prairies after he retired, documenting and photographing windmills, power mills, and water mills for the Alberta historical society," says Len, whose grandfather owned a windmill on his farm. "The society actually registered them all, but he was trying to convince someone or some organization to take on a project of ensuring that these things didn't eventually end up in a scrap heap. After the meeting, my wife and I looked at each other and we invited him over for coffee."

Bill was born on his family's homestead, 16 kilometres south of Etzikom, on August 26, 1911. His family, like many others in those pioneer days, was a victim of the wind-swept calamities of the era. In April 1922, Bill's older brother, George, became ill with appendicitis. He needed to go to a hospital, but a blizzard hit the area. Their parents, Will and Minnie, loaded the 12-year-old George on a sleigh, placed him on a bed of hay and covered him with warm blankets, and drove through drifting snow to Etzikom, hoping to reach Lethbridge.

Unfortunately, thick snow drifts blocked the rail tracks and George's arrival in Lethbridge was delayed. Although he underwent surgery, it was too late and he died.

Four years following George's death, the family moved to Vulcan. After finishing school, Bill took jobs all over Alberta and beyond. While on the road he combined his old passion for windmills with his newer passion for photography.

"I think it all stems from his grandfather's windmill," says Len. "It's a pyramid-shaped structure and power mill about 30 feet [about nine metres] tall, and today it's at the very centre of our windmill site." He adds, "Bill was a fanatical photographer and always said that a photograph wasn't worth taking if it wasn't captioned. Every picture he took he ran through his typewriter and added a caption on the back."

The 1988 meeting between the Mitzels and Bill went so well that it led to the opening of the Canadian National Historic Windpower Centre in 1990.

From 1988 to 2000, Bill and Len developed a close friendship and travelled extensively together to trade shows and conferences in Canada and the U.S. to promote their novel museum. Throughout the 1990s, Bill also continued his photography, stopping everywhere along country roads to take pictures of windmills. Future historians will never have any doubts about any details. "When they look at these pictures they will be able to turn them over and see on the back where they were taken, when they were shot, who took them, and who is standing in them," says Len. "It's all documented, and so is the scenery."

Illness forced to Bill to retire in 2000. Three years later he is still residing in Calgary. Len stays in contact with him and keeps him informed of new developments at the museum.

"Everywhere he went, he never ceased to speak about his birthplace of Etzikom, the windmills, the museum, and everything we have accomplished so far," says Len. "He was the best travelling advertisement that anyone or any place could possibly have."

Brooking, Saskatchewan
The Great Rabbit Drive

The morning light had not yet displayed its teeth above the horizon, but Richard Johnsrude was already convinced that March 13, 1934, was going to be a brilliantly beautiful day. Richard's upstairs room faced east, and the six-year-old could see from his window that it was calm, with the promise of a clear blue sky. However, it was still late winter and very cold. He could hear his father, Barney, downstairs, tossing wood into the stove to add more heat to the uninsulated house. His mother, Violet, was busy making the morning porridge. Mona, his younger sister, was beginning to stir.

It would be a while yet before his home was comfortably warm. Richard stayed in bed under his heavy down comforter a little while longer.

On winter days when Richard didn't have to go to school, he would head to the top of the small hill near town to ski. His dad had handcrafted a pair of skis for him and he enjoyed racing down the hill to the bank of a small creek. During the summers, he also spent many lazy days there. The leisurely swims in the cool water of the creek were a welcome relief from the region's blistering hot days — weather that devastated southern Saskatchewan in the 1930s. Sometimes he would meet Pete, a nice old bachelor rancher who picked the willows by the creek and wove baskets. One time Pete made one for Richard's mother, a basket she still owned 60 years later.

Normally, very little of consequence happened in the hamlet of Brooking, Saskatchewan. It was a small pioneer railway community with a population of about 50, located fewer than 25 kilometres south of the present-day Red Coat Trail, between Radville in the east and Ceylon in the west. Although it was first permanently settled at the beginning of the 20th century, the area directly south and extending to the border was well known by Canadian and American law enforcement officials in the final years of the 1880s. A border camp 60 kilometres southwest of Brooking, which later became a North West Mounted Police post called Big Muddy, was the reputed Canadian getaway hang-out for many outlaws, including Butch Cassidy and the Sundance Kid. The Big Muddy was the first northern station of what became known as the Outlaw Trails, a series of escape routes starting inside the Canadian border and weaving south to Mexico. The route was first started by Cassidy and had stations set up every 20 to 25 kilometres to offer outlaws fresh horses and supplies that could be purchased as needed.

Although Cassidy (whose real name was Robert Leroy Parker) and the Sundance Kid (Harry Longbaugh) were dead by 1922, the Big Muddy post remained open to police until 1930, because the Outlaw Trails had also become a rum-running route during prohibition.

In the late 1890s, a settler by the name of A.A. Johnson set up the first homestead at what was to become the hamlet of Brooking. When the railroad came through in 1910, he sold part of his farm for the new townsite. It was briefly called Stowes, after famed American writer Harriet Beecher Stowe, author of *Uncle Tom's Cabin*. However, local rancher Lawrence Haden, who came from the South Dakota community of Brookings, suggested his former community's name instead (but without the "s"). A.A. was outvoted and Brooking it was.

Five years earlier, in 1905, settlers in the area enjoyed the distinction of having the first cement bridge built in the province, west of the future townsite across Gibson Creek. It was a bridge that Richard swam under many times.

By 1934, the Depression had gripped everyone on the prairies. The land was ravaged by severe summer dust storms and drought. The sloughs, ponds, and dugouts were all dried up. Crops never had a chance when the dust storms blew all day and continued through the night. Many ranchers shipped their cattle herds to communal pastures and fields to avoid losing all their livestock. Basic farming became impossible and financial disaster followed. Many Brooking-area residents went bankrupt and were forced to pack up and look for work elsewhere. Most of the people who remained received government relief. Barney Johnsrude's family may have been poor, but at least he was working. They were better off than most.

One of Richard's most vivid and lasting images of Brooking, which had become his home in 1933, was the Russian thistle. It was a spiny weed that took hold in the stricken grassless meadows and pastures. Because of the lack of traditional feed in recent years, many farmers had no choice but to give their livestock Russian thistle, which was abundant.

The Great Rabbit Drive

When the wind blew through the hamlet's tiny Main Street, Russian thistles tumbled past the general store and finally out of sight until the next gust grabbed a score more.

"Thistles were always piling up against the fences, just like walls around a castle," remembers Richard almost 70 years later.

He also never forgot the rabbits. They were everywhere, multiplying across every meadow and acreage in the region, and especially on nearby pastures where the land was rough, thorny, and hummocky. The rabbit population ballooned into the hundreds of thousands in that part of Saskatchewan. It wasn't long before the creatures became a menace to the farm community.

"Fields would just move with them, and they were huge," says Richard, "eating anything. There were bounties on their skins, and we used to eat them all the time."

On that late winter day in March 1934, rabbits were on Barney's mind. For the past six weeks, he had been rallying folks from all over the district to participate in Brooking's Great Rabbit Drive. The struggling hamlet needed a community hall, but nobody – including the government – had any money. On most Sundays during the winter months, groups of residents, using bobsleighs, went on rabbit shoots, partly to cut down on the growing numbers in the region and partly because the animals had become a regular part of everybody's diet during the Depression.

The community club decided it would be a good idea to raise funds for the hall by having a rabbit hunt on a large scale. Barney, a Saskatchewan Wheat Pool grain buyer and Consumer Co-operative organizer, was chosen chairman of the Great Rabbit Drive committee. A Norwegian immigrant, he was a strong union man and member of the Cooperative Commonwealth Federation (CCF), Canada's first national socialist party.

Barney held dozens of meetings to plan the rabbit drive down to the finest detail. It was agreed by club members that the drive should be organized as if it were a military operation. The site for the event was located outside of town in a five-square-kilometre pasture area. Club members built a round corral, about 12 metres in diameter, out of old fence posts and fox wire. As a means to direct the rabbits to the corral, a V-shaped drift fence was constructed. Each arm of the fence stretched out for up to a kilometre and a half into the pasture. At the outer ends, the fence had a gap of a half kilometre, funnelling together at the other end at the corral.

In the interests of being humane and ensuring everyone's safety, participants were not allowed to have guns, dogs, or clubs. "Anyone who came with a gun was relieved of it," recounted Barney years later. "In addition, there was a committee to see that all rabbits were killed as humanely as possible."

In charge of the field operation was the "general." Next in line were four field commanders, each in charge of four driving armies, approaching the field of operations from different directions.

The drive began shortly after day break. Richard headed out to an abandoned farmhouse about a kilometre and a half west of town that was picked as a starting point for the drive. Most of the community met there, as well as many other farmers and families from neighbouring hamlets and districts. An old stove was heated up and coffee was served before the men headed out to take up their positions in the field.

The general of the entire group stood on the highest knoll in the area. From that vantage point, he pulled out his binoculars to watch the progress of the armies, each of them starting from a point seven to eight kilometres away from the V-shaped field of operations. The general's job was to make sure the armies were operating in unison. He could use large flags to signal any of the advancing armies if they were moving too fast or too slow.

"When the armies were closing in, the whole side of the prairie hill was a moving mass of white — the colour rabbits turn in the wintertime," recalled Barney.

An estimated 3200 rabbits were driven into the corral, where assigned clubbers were stationed to kill them. Organizers wanted to skin the dead animals and sell the coats to fur buyers and the carcasses to a fox farm. However, with only 10 to 15 men to skin the animals before dark, it was an impossible task.

In the end, only 1200 pelts could be sold to fur buyers. The rest were handed over unskinned to the fox farm. Organizers earned a total gross of $600 towards the construction of a new community hall.

In subsequent years, there were other rabbit drives in the region, but none as well-organized as the 1934 event in Brooking. The community hall, however, never did get built. There was not enough other money available in those days to complete it.

While the Great Rabbit Drive gave residents of Brooking a brief diversion from the drudgery of the Depression, the effects didn't last. Brooking was never to live out its early promise. When the railroad first came through almost a quarter century earlier, it was predicted that the place would become the major town in the region. Canadian National Railway shops were planned, but were never realized because water supply in the area was poor. Instead, the railway company built its repair shop and roundhouse at Radville. As well, better roads allowed more people to travel and move to larger centres. Businesses also chose to go there, which slowly but surely doomed Brooking. It became a ghost town, leaving only the pioneer cement bridge as a reminder to visitors of the community.

Barney passed away in 1981 and Richard later became a country doctor in Saskatchewan. In the early 1960s he drove through the old area of his youth. "We drove through out of curiosity, but there was nothing there," recalls Richard.

As sad as it was to find out that Brooking had vanished, he recalls fondly his childhood days by the creek and his life growing up in the small community.

He also remembers well that day back in March 1934 when the town came together during the depths of the Depression to stage the Great Rabbit Drive. "It was a morale-boosting community effort at a time when nobody had any money," says Richard in 2003. "It was the greatest weekend I can remember when I was a kid."

Scotsguard, Saskatchewan
Little Chicago

I t was October 31, 1970, when a rash of reports to the Shaunavon RCMP detachment started coming in about strange doings near Scotsguard, a hamlet about 30 kilometres northeast of Shaunavon. It had been nearly a half a century since so much commotion had come out of the small town.

Callers were claiming that strange white figures were floating out of a cemetery, onto the highway, and into a ditch. This was a new twist for Scotsguard. The town did have an old reputation for wild living, but those were the days of the hell-raising '20s, when

Scotsguard was known as "Little Chicago." By 1970, Scotsguard had become a ghost town, far removed from the era of high-rolling card sharks and cowboy gun-slingers.

When Mounties arrived at the cemetery, it didn't take long to figure out that several young teens were wrapped in white sheets and dashing across the high-way, leaving surprised motorists with notions that ghosts were on the loose. Another Halloween prank.

The leading phantom was a Scotsguard girl, and the Mounties drove her back to town, where the streets were dark and quiet. They didn't, as they once might have, take her to the old jail in the back room of what used to be the fire hall, across the road from Island's Hardware Store.

It had been Little Chicago's "sin bin," where many a rabble rouser from days gone by spent the night after an evening of drunken debauchery. It was once the domain of Luke Willy, a large and stocky pioneer cop whose booming commands of law and order were respected by all in Scotsguard. During the 1920s, Luke was the law in Scotsguard, which never had its own RCMP or Saskatchewan Provincial Police detachment. A black-smith by profession, he also briefly went into partner-ship with two other locals to manufacture and patent a soap and cleaner out of lard called "Clean I Mean Soap."

The venture didn't last long and Luke resumed his law enforcement duties with his signature call, "Halt, in the name of the law!"

"Everyone respected Luke because he was a pretty husky guy. He never wore a uniform, but always had a billy club to scare us guys," says Bud Simmons, whose family first came to the Scotsguard area in 1912. "Luke made sure that it did not get too rowdy. Saturday nights would be his busiest time, or any other night that had a dance."

Little Chicago's notoriety grew at a time when bootleggers and rum-runners made small fortunes, fuelling the countless card sharks who blazed through town every payday for a weekend of high-stakes poker. Always following the bootleggers, however, was Luke, and maybe an eager policeman from another district.

"Apparently there was one lady in town known to be a bootlegger. The police wanted to catch her, so one day they decided to raid her place," says Keith Hagen, whose family roots in the Scotsguard area go back to 1919. "When they got in there, she said, 'Well, search the house.' She told the police she was too sick to get out of bed. They made their search, but couldn't find anything. It wasn't until much later they realized the woman was hiding the liquor with her in bed."

When settlers first arrived in the district a decade

earlier, it was not for the wild living and good times. Rather, it was for the free land for new homesteads promised by the government. But times were hard in the early years.

Before the railway came through in 1914, this was just another place on the map that was a destination for scores of settlers who ventured west with the hopes of a new and better life. The settlement was originally called Notukeu, but was changed to Scotsguard in 1914 after someone realized there was another town in the province with the same name. A homesteader, Ed Smith, christened the new community Scotsguard because of his claims of having been a Scots guard during his youth. By 1916, Scotsguard's population was just over 100, enough to qualify it for legal incorporation as a village.

The first few years were often hard for settlers. The weather was dry, crops were poor, and there was little or no money. During one bleak year, the new village was on the verge of bankruptcy, with only one cent cash on hand and uncollected taxes totalling more than $700. Luckily, the good times started to roll for Scotsguard in the 1920s, and the town's population peaked at 350. A building boom resulted in the construction of numerous new businesses, including six grain elevators, restaurants, garages, hardware stores, a theatre, a bank, a municipal office, and hotel.

Cattle ranchers were also doing well in the area. Scotsguard had the largest stockyards west of Moose Jaw at one time, with thousands of head of cattle shipped out every autumn.

"We used to sit on the fence and watch the cattle coming in," says Bud. "There was a lot of gambling, pool playing, and drinking. Scotsguard was popular with the cowboys because of all the ranching in the area. In fact, they'd ride their horses right into the pool hall."

As the town prospered, so too did the farmers. The harvests improved and farmers had more money to spend. It became an everyday sight to see farmers come into Scotsguard, unload their wheat, and head to the backs of either the cafés or the hotel to spend their hard-earned cash.

This was the beginning of an exciting era for the town, and the boom attracted scores of new people. However, prosperity always attracts renegades who want some of the action. Scotsguard was no different and the billy-club-wielding Luke Willy was kept busy.

John Goodman's general store was once held up by a gunman who robbed the clerk of cash. John was also the victim of another heist when burglars broke into the store one night and blew open the safe. The robbers stole all of Goodman's cash, as well as money owned by the pool elevator company.

Little Chicago

The booming economy also created a greater demand for hired help. In particular, more men were needed for the fall harvests, and threshing crews were hired from as far away as Ontario and the United States. Some of the crews employed up to 20 men, working with little rest from daylight to dark for almost three weeks. A team of horses dragged around a bunkhouse and cookhouse for the hungry and weary men. When the harvest was over, the crews needed to unwind — and it wasn't long into the Roaring Twenties when Scotsguard became dubbed Little Chicago. Prohibition, rum-running, and bootlegging flourished. Poker games were played out round the clock.

"They [the threshing crews] came to town and got hooked up to play poker because they wanted to make big money before they went home. They weren't fussy about the night of the week," says Jalmar Torwick, who was born in the Scotsguard area in 1918. "A lot of times they would be upstairs in the pool hall, in a room where they could play as long as they wanted. There used to be poker pots in the thousands of dollars. A lot of the guys would go broke and would have to stay around here for a while afterwards."

As it turned out, the crews didn't stay long. By the end of the 1920s the worldwide Depression had started, and on its heels drought and sand storms arrived in the region. The good harvest years were over and it signalled the end of Scotsguard's glory days. Little Chicago became little more than a memory, as fewer and fewer locals came to town to spend money. There was less work to do and crews stopped coming from the east. Many poverty-stricken bachelors were forced to live on a monthly relief cheque of $4.20.

When the dust bowl days finally started to subside during the early years of World War II, Scotsguard was dealt another blow. A fire in 1941 ripped through 11 buildings along the north side of Main Street, destroying the pool hall, the Grill Café, Eddie's Lunch, the post office, and the Beaver Lumber Company. The only building saved was John Goodman's hotel. Locals who relied on the town's dwindling services were fortunate because the hotel also housed a barber shop, confectionary, beer parlour, and pool hall. The entire business section would have been destroyed if not for the heroic efforts of John and his family. They risked serious injury and even death by climbing to the roof tops of threatened buildings to put out sparks with wet rags.

Scotsguard never recovered from the blaze. The municipal office moved to Instow, 13 kilometres west, and 15 families moved their belongings and homes out of town.

John, who also lost a grocery store in the fire of

1918, sold the hotel in 1946, but not before witnessing one of the town's more bizarre moments. Ole Aastad, who owned the hotel before John, came into the pool hall one night and was challenged to a $5 wager that he could not put a pool ball in his mouth. Ole accepted the challenge, opened wide, and pushed in the ball. He won his bet. Unfortunately, though, he couldn't get the ball out, even with the help of alarmed hall patrons. He was driven to Shaunavon where a doctor managed to extract the ball from his well-stretched mouth. From then on, Ole kept his wagering to the pool table.

Throughout the rest of the 1940s and into the 1950s, a steady flow of citizens left Scotsguard. With the population in decline, locals agreed that the town as a legal entity was no longer viable. It was dissolved as a village on December 31, 1953. Less than six months later, fire destroyed the hotel.

Keith Hagen was a five-year-old living on a farm six kilometres east of Scotsguard when the official death of the town was announced. In the mid-1960s he left the area to embark on a career as an accountant. After living and working in Brooks, Alberta, for 15 years, he returned with his family to Scotsguard in 1987. The town, which once held so much promise for countless people, was a shell of its former self. Only seven residents remained.

Keith bought a house there and moved in anyway,

soon rekindling his long fascination with history, starting with the restoration of several antique cars.

"I built a garage behind our house to work on these old cars. As I got some finished, I began to wonder where I could store them," says Keith, who now has an accounting practice in Shaunavon. "Different old buildings were just sitting there empty, so I figured why not use them for storage. I went through whatever channels I needed to get them."

Over the years, Keith has bought and restored most of the town's remaining pioneer buildings, including the old United Church, fire hall and jail, and curling rink. He and his wife are the last residents of Scotsguard, and loving it.

"In most cases, paying off taxes or giving a donation to the church and paying for the transfer fees were all it took to acquire the structures," says Keith, who also farms several hundred acres of land adjacent to the townsite.

"I've got lots of room here, and don't feel lonesome at all," he adds. "It's great, especially in the evening and the early morning. You go outside and walk down Main Street and the birds are singing and the bush rabbits are running."

His ongoing private restoration project of the town has included putting up replicas of Scotsguard's pioneer street signs at every corner and planting almost 100 evergreens around the townsite. In summertime, it is not uncommon to see Keith mowing the lawns of properties that were once the sites of pioneer businesses and families from the town's Little Chicago days.

"When I was turning up a little bit of land at the edge of Scotsguard, I found a sign that says 'Speed Limit 20 miles per hour by Police Order,' so I definitely have to put that up," says Keith, who receives many sightseers from spring to fall.

He also plans on rescuing part of the old Lutheran church from Simmie, a fading community north of Scotsguard. However, he insists the town he now almost completely owns will not become a final resting place for all ghost town memorabilia.

"I don't think so. I keep telling myself this is it," says Keith, "but I still need more storage. Can you believe that?"

Ravenscrag, Saskatchewan
Family Affair

hile standing near the intersection of Wall Street and Railway Avenue in Ravenscrag, Cliff Arnal is explaining his hometown's history to a Montreal film crew when a sudden rush of wind rattles the windows of a dilapidated building nearby. A second gust slams the structure's front door open and shut. The three visitors from Quebec turn their backs and grimace as dust is swept into their faces, momentarily blinding them.

It does not go unnoticed by the crew that this storm displayed its ferocity only mere minutes after their arrival to film a segment for a ghost town documentary.

Family Affair

Ravenscrag is such a town, a forlorn place that can easily be described as haunting. It is isolated, sitting well off the main highway; and stark and lonely. The town, once home to about 200 people in the 1920s, now has only 18 diehard residents. Seventeen of them are from Cliff's family, and Cliff is head of the unofficial welcoming committee.

The film crew has never before visited Saskatchewan, but their anxiety is relieved somewhat by a faint sense of familiarity. They soon learn that the history of this once proud community — a ghost town for the past several decades — has a pronounced French influence. Their charming and gracious host can also claim French heritage.

When the wind subsides, Cliff smiles at his three young French-Canadian guests, repositions his ball cap, and continues his tour along Wall Street, where a row of businesses once stood. The visitors have been told the town, nestled alongside the Frenchman River at the bottom of Blacktail Coulee, received its name in 1914 from a Canadian Pacific Railway employee. The railway company had recently purchased a large ocean liner company from shipping magnate Sir Hugh Allan. The mansion that Sir Hugh built in Montreal in 1881 was named Ravenscrag.

The CPR, meanwhile, decided to push its rail line

to this corner of southwestern Saskatchewan during a visit to the area in 1912. Company officials discovered that the first homesteader, Spencer Pearce, had settled in the area in 1890. Spencer named his homestead Point View. The CPR renamed the townsite Ravenscrag and within 20 years scores of settlers had followed Pearce's lead.

England native Frank Barroby first set his eyes on the area in 1901. It was the same spot where the future townsite of Ravenscrag would be built. He was moved by the country's unspoiled beauty: "Little did I think there would ever be a townsite anywhere in this district. To me this area was wonderfully picturesque, its deep coulees filled with spruce and cottonwoods, its lovely creeks rippling with cool water, its thousands of acres of well-grassed land, its abundance of hay and shelter, and scarcely a furrow turned."

Cliff's grandparents, Louis and Germaine, arrived at about the same time Frank did to the same beautiful spot along the Frenchman River, coming by wagon and a team of oxen in October 1909. The couple spoke very little English. They originally came to Canada from northern Algeria. The elder Arnal's first home in this strange new land was a sod shack 16 kilometres north of where the town was eventually built. They later con-structed a log house, and then in 1929 moved to a larger house, which is still standing on the original homestead.

"There is quite a story behind that house, because with the stock market crash in 1929, the Arnals ended up selling a bunch of grain for 10 cents a bushel to finish that house" says Cliff. "People lived in it until 1975. When we have family reunions, descendants come down here. It's kind of home for them all."

The affable Cliff is a natural storyteller. He recalls a remarkable tale about his grandfather, Louis, told to him decades ago by Frank Barroby. Apparently, Louis used to work away from home for days at a time for a French count. He bought a horse from a local rancher because his wife and their new baby, Clément, had no transportation. Not long after securing the horse, an odd thing occurred. Louis was away on business one day when he noticed a supply wagon bringing in a shipment of goods for the Count. One of the horses looked very familiar — too familiar, in fact.

"He helped the wagon driver unload and asked him where he got the horse in question," says Cliff. "My grandfather was pretty upset because he'd already figured out what had happened. The horse he'd just bought for his wife had been stolen — and this was it, resold to the supply wagon fellow already. That evening he told the Count he had to go home."

On his way back to his homestead, Louis made a

detour to the home of the rancher who sold him his horse. The two argued and a fist fight ensued, which the elder Arnal was winning due to his past training in the French army. The rancher's wife, fearing for her husband's life, picked up a fence post and headed towards the irate Algerian to break up the fight.

"My grandfather saw it coming just as she was swinging, and she swung it pretty heavy," says Cliff. "She connected — on her husband's head — and knocked him out! A hired hand saw this all happen and of course the fight ended."

Louis left the scene and went home. After a few minutes of standing over his unconscious ranch boss, the hired hand grew concerned. He saddled up his horse and road eight kilometres into the valley towards Frank's spread. The hand told Frank what had happened and they rode back to the ranch where the stunned owner finally came to, a little humiliated but not seriously hurt.

"My grandfather never did get the horse back," says Cliff.

Back on Cliff's tour with the Montreal film crew, the wind is once again picking up strength. Cliff is showing his guests the site of the former Ravenscrag Hotel, built by John Kalk in 1915. It was destroyed, along with many other businesses, by a ferocious wind-swept fire in 1954. The fire was considered the death blow for the town, which had been in serious decline since the late 1920s.

"There was a lot of confusion, a lot of wind," says Cliff, who was eight years old at the time of the fire. "They let the school out because the kids could not concentrate on what they were doing."

As with many pioneer communities, the hotel was the focal point of Ravenscrag's social life and the scene of many wild capers over the years. With a wide grin, Cliff recounts a famous 1930s Ravenscrag tale.

"A couple of guys decided they were going to have some fun, and they moved the hotel outhouse back past the hole," says Cliff. "Then they watched to see who was going to go into it, and this older man eventually did. When he came back into the hotel he was cussing. A few patrons asked him why he was swearing," Cliff continues. "He cussed some more and shot back, 'Can't you smell? I fell in the hole!'"

As the group follows Cliff down Railway Avenue, they come to the remnants of the last grain elevator, which was demolished in 1987 or 1988. When it was toppled, it landed upside down. The town's name is still visible on the side — also upside down.

The topic of grain elevators is a passionate one for Cliff, as it is for many farmers in rural Saskatchewan. Since the 1980s, hundreds of old wooden grain elevators in the province, as well as in other provinces in western

Canada, have fallen. The relics became victims of the changing times as rail lines began to close and grain-handling operations were consolidated into much larger and faster concrete terminals.

It's always an emotional moment when a grain company announces the closure of an elevator in a rural Saskatchewan community. And it was no different for folks in and around Ravenscrag in the early 1980s when it was first announced their elevators were going to be demolished.

"The company's policy at the time was that no elevator could stay standing because then the company had to pay the taxes on it," says Cliff. "There was a meeting about it, but company people said that the only way we could keep one elevator open was if we had a petition signed by all the people who supported it. Ninety-nine percent of the people who were available signed a petition against demolition, but it got destroyed anyway. The petition ended up being a waste of time. There was a great deal of bitterness about it, and a lot of people boycotted the company because of it."

When the last elevator in Ravenscrag fell in the late 1980s, life changed dramatically for all local farmers. Cliff, for instance, used to haul two truckloads an hour to the local elevator. The next closest grain elevators were about an hour's drive away, in Eastend, Robsart, and Maple Creek. This meant that farmers had to start days as early as 4 a.m. to maintain competitive production levels. Aside from the extra time on the road, the added fuel costs for long distance deliveries increased the financial woes of many farmers.

In March 2000, the Saskatchewan Wheat Pool put the finishing touches on its new concrete inland terminal in Maple Creek. The company wanted a true pioneer ceremonial inauguration for the new facility's grand opening, which was set for July. Officials also believed the special opening should be hosted by local farmers. As well, they liked the idea of a grand opening that featured a load of grain being hauled into the new terminal the same way farmers used to bring wheat into town in the pioneer days — by horse and wagon. Well aware of the Arnals' long history in the region, the company asked Cliff if he would haul in a wagon full of wheat for the event.

Cliff was enthusiastic about the concept, but insisted that the first official load should be the first load ever, and be delivered on April 1.

"One of the fellows in charge said that if I wanted to bring in the first load, I'd be welcome to it. The problem was that by this time I only had three weeks to get everything ready. I had no team and no wagon," says Cliff "but I guess I liked the challenge."

The project became a third-, fourth-, and fifth-generation family affair, including brother Clarence and son Frank who played key roles. Cliff managed to secure a wooden wheel wagon from a friend in Scotsguard, which needed extensive work. After about a week's labour by family members and friends, the wagon was ready. Cliff didn't have any trained heavy horses for the 60-kilometre trip, but Frank supplied a pair of saddle horses: a 955-pound palomino mare named Barbie and a 960-pound Arabian stallion named Sky. The pair's job was to pull a wagon loaded with wheat — a total load weighing 3849 pounds from Ravenscrag to Maple Creek.

Everyone involved in the project knew that training saddle horses that had never been harnessed for this type of job would be a monumental task. With time running out, Cliff and his helpers had only 24 hours to get the new team to work. Cliff was also aware that the horses were not big enough or strong enough for the rough ride ahead over hills and rough rural prairie roads. He decided that they would get regular rest during the journey.

The trip took several days. "We went home every night. I left the wagon on the side of the road, and we put the horses in the trailer and drove them home," says Cliff. "We didn't have to, but it was easier than hauling their feed and so forth, so we just took the horses home and fed them there."

Braving cold and windy spring weather, with snow and rain, it took 17 hours and 30 minutes of travelling time to bring in the wagon on April 1. The saddle horses were up for the job, even if they needed a little bit of coaxing as they got close to Maple Creek.

Immediately following the historic journey, a sample of grain was handed over to the grain company and to the museum in Maple Creek. Clifford also kept a sample for himself. The grain company gave him the customary $90 grain cheque for his delivery, but he has never cashed it. The cheque is framed and hangs in the office of the inland terminal. Cliff made it officially into the record books.

After the brief tour of Ravenscrag's fading townsite, Cliff invites his guests home, a welcome chance for everyone to get out of the cold and wind. He brings out his country fiddle and offers the visitors a rendition of *White River Stump*, a traditional folk song. He also plays a bluegrass tune called *Underneath the Double Eagle*. His audience listens respectfully as Cliff transports them back to an era when French pioneers integrated with western Canadian culture.

Cliff knows Ravenscrag is not what it used to be. Still, he's proud of his town's prosperous roots. "Residents were honoured to live under the shadows of those once great grain elevators," he says. In the meantime, Ravenscrag hangs on, with Cliff and his family as its last proud caretakers.

Robsart, Saskatchewan
Ghosts and Renegades

Every once in a while, Archie Smiley still goes back to his hometown to look around the old hospital where he was born on December 31, 1917. But he can no longer go inside the derelict Robsart landmark. The only access to the hospital is from the main road going into town, and one has to either crawl under a barbed-wire fence or climb over it. Even if these exertions were possible for Archie, the front porch leading to the entrance was removed long ago — creating a challenging climb for anyone, never mind an 86-year-old retiree.

The two-storey building was closed as a hospital

Archie Smiley in front of the Robsart Hospital in late 2000. He
was born in the building on December 31, 1917.

several decades ago and abandoned as a residence in
the 1960s. It stands stark and lonely in what is now a
ghost town.

Brisk prairie winds constantly blast through the blown-out windows, swirling around the empty rooms. Once in a while, startled pigeons scatter. There is even an occasional hoot from an owl, resting somewhere up in the second floor.

"I was born in the room right over there," says Archie, pointing towards a smashed-out window. "It was a tough winter, I'm told. When my father, Joe, took us home to the farm, it took five hours to go about 12 miles north of Robsart."

Now, all that remains of the Smiley homestead are a few 20-metre poplar trees. In Robsart, there are more tangible reminders of a populated past, but these are punctuated with an overwhelming feeling of abandonment. The pioneer town's once magnificent business section now looks like a classic postcard of ghost towns in southwestern Saskatchewan. Both sides of Main Street are lined by abandoned buildings with weathered false fronts, boarded up doors, and cracked windows. On the north side of town, several residences sit empty. No one walks or plays by these homes anymore.

Fewer than half a dozen residents remain in town, hanging on to the last flickering hope that the old community can survive. Some people still work in the area, and a few are retired.

"It was a busy town at one time, with lots of

activity," says Archie, who left Robsart in 1998 to retire to Maple Creek, about 80 kilometres north. "It's now kind of a sad thing, but a sign of the times. People ask me, 'Do you miss Robsart?' and I say, 'There is nothing to miss now.'"

Ninety years ago, in 1913, Archie's family trekked to the desolate southwest corner of the province after six hard years of pioneer living in North Dakota. His parents, Joe and Hattie Smiley, were originally from Nova Scotia. They were struck with the "Go West" fever that consumed countless others during the 20th century's last great land rush.

In 1910, the Canadian Pacific Railway purchased a quarter section of land in the southwest corner of the province and named it Robsart — after Amy Robsart, the heroine in Sir Walter Scott's novel *Kenilworth*. Three years later, Henry Abbott led the first pioneer settlers, including the Smileys, to the new prairie community and quickly built a general store and feed mill. Soon the new town had a mayor, council, town hall, and more than 30 businesses and services, including a dentist and veterinary surgeon.

The arrival of the railway in 1914 really got things going. Every week, locals observed, fresh businesses opened their doors. There were new hotels, cafés, livery barns, grain elevators, a bank, churches, a school, and even a photography store run by Uncle John Asplund. And, of course, there was the hospital, opening in 1916 and delivering Archie Smiley to the world the following year. Within a decade of its humble beginnings, Robsart had a population of 350.

Joe and Hattie arrived in Saskatchewan by train. As the rail line to Robsart was not yet finished, the couple, along with two young daughters, had to disembark in Maple Creek with all their belongings. From there, they were going to make the arduous horse-and-buggy trek to their land claim north of Robsart.

"My husband and another man who had come with us unloaded the cars. There was no place where they could store the goods, so they piled them beside the stock yards," says Hattie. "They began to haul some of our possessions, together with our stock, out to our claim. While they were gone with lumber for our buildings, a lot of our goods were stolen."

The Smileys quickly put the unpleasant experience behind them and continued their journey, across barely discernible prairie trails to get to their promised land. When they arrived at their claim, they lived in a loaned two-room ranch house, with a lean-to attached to the building for the stock and chickens.

The family soon learned about the land's dry and unforgiving climate, when the following summer yielded no crops on their barely broken acreage. The harvest was so grim that the family went back to North Dakota for the rest of the year to take advantage of the bounty of their former land. They did not return to Saskatchewan again until the spring of 1915. Their fortunes improved that year, but there were more challenging times ahead as they battled with the unpredictable elements.

January 10, 1916, began as a beautiful and mild day. Hattie remembers being able to stay outside for "quite awhile" that morning without a coat. A neighbour, Gordon Pack, had come by the evening before and played cards with Joe until the early hours of the morning. He had stayed the night and Hattie was up early to make breakfast. Then came the wind, so strong the entire house creaked and groaned.

"This woke up the men and they came down to see what was going on," says Hattie. "When they went out, it was commencing to snow and they saw the horses coming on the run for the barn. The blizzard became so bad, the men could scarcely get back to the house."

Battling hurricane-like winds, Joe and Gordon struggled to find some large poles and propped them against the house, three on the outside and two inside. However, it was clear that the storm was winning the battle and the house began to sag under the force of the wind. Hattie nailed quilts and blankets across the doorway to shut out the draft, but it did little to keep out the cold.

"The men brought in all the fuel they could and we had two ripping fires on and the stoves were red hot, yet it was so cold we could hardly tell there was any fire," Hattie remembers.

The blizzard lasted three days. For most of the first day, Hattie and her daughters stayed in the cellar. The only time she felt warm was when she tried to cook. But her feet were frozen, even with her overshoes on. Gordon stayed until the afternoon of the third day. When the storm finally subsided, the house was still standing, albeit it askew. Joe straightened it out with a jack.

There would be more hard winters ahead, including the one in 1917 when Archie was born.

Joe supplemented his meagre farm income with blacksmithing and general handyman jobs throughout the district, but times remained difficult for the next decade. The land was too rocky and never produced a good crop. This, combined with Joe and Hattie's desire to give their children an education, prompted them to move into Robsart in 1928.

Robsart was still enjoying prosperity. Postcards and the new local newspaper, *The Messenger*, even boasted that Robsart was "the town with a bright future." But many residents throughout the district, including the Smileys, continued to struggle to make ends meet. A few people resorted to extreme measures, which sometimes led to intrigue, crime, and even murder.

Archie remembers the strange tale of Dave Greenwood, a prohibition rum-runner who lived in the area during the 1920s. Dave was known as a private man who kept beautiful large horses on his acreage. In 1918, he bought the first tractor in the district — but that, along with the fact that he had a wife and daughter in Montana, was about all that people knew about him.

"Quite a few cars went through Robsart in those days headed for Chinook, Montana. They were running rum," recalls Archie of those times. "On one particular night, Dave arrived at our place in his dad's car, a Dodge roadster. We found out it was loaded with whiskey."

The following morning, Dave went to leave, but the car's engine wouldn't turn over in the cold weather. After several laboured turns with the crank, the car eventually started but the water pump shaft broke. Handyman Joe quickly built a new shaft. "Dave was so happy," recalls Archie, "that he gave each one of us kids some money. I got $10 and my sisters each got $20. That was big money back then."

Dave was never seen again.

Although Joe and many others later tried to find

out what happened to him, they learned little. Even his daughter, Grace, wrote to every prison in the U.S. to see if her father had ended up there, but to no avail. Many years later, she received a telegraph from Wyoming police telling her Dave was ill with pneumonia and not expected to live. She set out to see her long-lost father, but shortly before she left, an unidentified man telephoned and told her Dave had passed away.

When Grace tried to contact the hospital that was supposedly caring for her father, she discovered there was no such institution. She also found out that the cemetery where Dave was allegedly buried didn't even exist. The same caller who told her that her father had passed away also mentioned a bottling works company that Dave purportedly held a partnership in. Such a company didn't exist either.

Despite Grace's continued efforts to clear up the mystery, she never found any new leads. Many years later, however, her daughter, California native Haylene Abner, received a completely unexpected letter not long after she had made a visit to Canada. The letter asked her to contact the RCMP in Maple Creek because her late grandfather — Dave Greenwood — had left her $222 in a local bank. The family contacted the RCMP, only to find someone else had access to the money and it was gone. To this day, the fate of Dave

Greenwood remains a dark mystery.

When the stock market crashed in 1929, the Smileys and everyone else in the Robsart area were forced to cope with the fallout. The bleak '30s followed. A Thanksgiving fire in 1930 added to the town's woes, wiping out most of the business core.

The Depression years, together with droughts, falling grain prices, and poor crop yields, completed the devastation. Most merchants, staggering under heavy financial losses, packed up and left. Many locals stayed and eked out a living, but it was often next to impossible for some people to cope with the never-ending calamities and reverses of fortune.

"We knew this old rancher in 1931," says Archie, "who decided to shoot himself. Nobody knows really why he did, but they figured he couldn't take it anymore. He'd always had a little money, but in 1931 it was very dry, and he must have worried about getting feed for his cattle."

By 1938, Depression living became too much for the Smiley family. After receiving government assistance, they moved back to Nova Scotia. The family survived there by working at odd jobs and taking advantage of the plentiful low-priced fruit and vegetables. For a few years they travelled back and forth to the prairies for the autumn harvest, but ultimately they decided to return to Robsart permanently. It was home, and they would make the best of it.

Archie helped support his family by working at odd jobs. He also took up playing the country fiddle in 1934 while recovering from the mumps.

Even though the hardships of the Depression were easing with the advent of World War II, it was tough for Archie to earn a living in his hometown. He and his father went to Medicine Hat and even to Vancouver for work, but always returned to Robsart. Archie eventually worked for the railway and made a little extra playing the fiddle. He married a school teacher from the Vidora district.

Archie remained active in community affairs for the next half century, including serving as the last mayor of Robsart from 1978 to 1991. In his spare time back then, he fixed antique cars, restored fiddles, and played his down-home music to delighted locals for more than 55 years. During his working years as a grain buyer, he also took up a serious interest in restoring antique clocks.

"One time I had 16 of them in the elevator office. All were in running order," says Archie.

Archie has more time than ever now to do whatever he wishes, including making occasional visits to Robsart, even though these trips bring sadness. Before he left the town in the 1990s, Archie made several contributions to a local history book project. He thought it important that people never forget his beloved Robsart, and the way its pioneer citizens persevered through crises.

One of Archie's last gifts to the town was a modified poem called "Ode to Robsart," which he did for a community history book.

Here's to Robsart, it's still here yet,
No store, no hotel, a well with a jet.
The main street still stretching, not much in
your way.
When you put it together, there is nothing more,
No hustle, no bustle, no rumble, no roar.
It's as dead as a doornail, it's old as the hills,
No fun, no excitement, no jolly old thrills.
But still we did love it, though far we may roam,
For Robsart is Robsart, and Robsart was home.

Vidora, Saskatchewan
Box Car Adventures

s Charles Behrman loaded up his belongings and family for the journey from Vidora to Shaunavon, he couldn't help but wonder about the trails he had already travelled during his young life. It was the winter of 1941 and he was 33 years old. He could look anyone in the eye and say with complete honesty that his life up to that point had been filled with more adventures than most men twice his age had experienced. But now he had a family and it was time to leave the town of Vidora. The Depression had worn him down and he was going to begin a new life in Shaunavon with his own implement business.

"Roads were terrible in those days, and most of my driving was on the prairie trails and pastures," says Charles, who was a horse buyer in the mid- to late 1930s and early '40s. He was a man of the road in his professional life, having travelled extensively by auto throughout southwest Saskatchewan and southern Alberta. "I had to buy a new car every year. At 30,000 miles they were worn out."

The journey from his farm near Vidora to Shaunavon was more than 100 kilometres. Shaunavon was faring better than most communities along Highway 13, particularly during the war years. However, the town was still reeling from the slaying of an RCMP sergeant, Arthur Barker, the year before.

Charles knew the family of the killer, Victor Greenlay, and was shocked by the news.

"It happened in that big hotel here in Shaunavon, the one that has been vacant for 20 or 30 years," remembers Charles in 2003. "The guy, Victor, shot and killed the Mountie on the stairs."

It was a killing that rocked every community in the Red Coat Trail region. Arthur and Victor had been good friends. Victor was the 31-year-old son of Gardner Greenlay, a prominent Lieutenant-Colonel in the 14th Saskatchewan Light Horse and former sergeant with the North West Mounted Police.

Victor was a deeply troubled man and Arthur agreed to meet him during the evening of March 16, 1940, at Shaunavon's Grand Hotel. The Mountie listened to his friend's incoherent ramblings for about two hours. Minutes after Arthur left Victor's room, the disturbed man followed him to the lobby and shot him three times with a .38 revolver. Arthur was killed instantly, leaving behind a wife, Gladys, and their seven-year-old son, Kenneth.

When Charles drove away from Vidora, he was also leaving behind his past trials, although these later served to be a great source of strength in the days and years ahead.

He was born in Stoughton, Saskatchewan, in 1908 and moved with his family two years later to the Vidora district in southwest Saskatchewan. The village of Vidora, located between Robsart and Consul, was established in 1914 when the Canadian Pacific Railway was under construction in the area. The new settlement was named after two nearby farm girls, Vi and Dora, who lived at a farmhouse that also housed CPR engineers and surveyors during the rail line's construction.

Like most towns in the area at the time, Vidora grew quickly. By the early 1920s, the town boasted a population of about 200 and had more than 20 businesses, including two banks, lumber yards, a hotel, and five grain elevators. Vidora was also active socially, with numerous church and school programs and annual summer fairs. A 30-piece band was organized during Vidora's heyday, and for several years it played at picnics and special events, including a "Bootleggers Ball" in Govenlock when that town was renowned for its nefarious ways (see "No-Guff Gaff").

It appeared Vidora's future was indeed worthy of celebration. But there were disturbing signs of things to come. A fire in 1924 destroyed a good part of the town's business section, including the post office, a store, a café, and a pool hall. Another blaze struck in 1926 and one more in 1928, both claiming several more businesses and services. No other pioneer town along the Red Coat Trail in Saskatchewan suffered as much as Vidora when it came to fires.

"I was seven years old at the time of the fire in 1924," says Wilson Swihart, who grew up on a farm a kilometre and a half north of the townsite. "It destroyed most of what was on the west side of the street. I remember clearly the general store burning down. I could hear the canned goods exploding.

"Us kids went after school and rummaged around through the piles of ashes after the fire and we found a .38 automatic handgun, but it was ruined," Wilson recounts. "We were still fascinated with it, although it was of no possible use — just a curiosity. My older brother oiled it all up and hammered on it. He eventually got it working enough to eject an empty shell."

While the series of fires devastated the community, Vidora was already under economic pressure in the late 1920s as a result of a series of poor harvests. Most citizens were living a marginal existence. Jobs were scarce and many men and their families were already looking to leave the town for a better life elsewhere.

In 1928, Charles was fresh out of a college program at Melville, Saskatchewan. He went home to his family farm, just south of Vidora, to decide his future. His main interests at that time were coyote hunting and chasing girls. "I thought I knew everything," he says.

After working one autumn in the hay fields near Vidora, he moved on to try a few jobs in the big city of Regina, but no situation worked out. He was fired from at least two jobs and then became ill with the mumps. After a few weeks of recovery, he hopped on the first westbound train back to Vidora, where he settled back into the comforts of his family home.

Next he tried his luck at homesteading, securing 160 acres of farmland near Vidora. His first year went well, but drought struck in the fall of 1929, virtually ruining the harvest. He decided to leave his hometown again and this time determined more than ever to prove to everybody he could make the big time all by himself. He began a year-long odyssey that took him to the deepest depths of despair. He experienced more misfortune than any young man from the Red Coat Trail region would endure during the first dark year of the Depression.

Charles decided to go with his brother Bob and cousin Fred to Kindersley, Saskatchewan, to look for work. After a 130-kilometre trip, the trio immediately found a place to stay above the town's White Spot Café and were hired the following morning to work in the fields. Next day, however, a snowstorm blew over the area, putting a halt to any field work for at least a few weeks. After seeing the trio hanging around Kindersley for a while with no money or work, the owner of the White Spot presented them with a business opportunity.

As Charles recalls it, "She said, 'I'll sell you this café and give you a good deal. All you have to pay down is a thousand dollars and the same amount every six months until it's paid for.'"

This was too good to be true. The café was booming, with local railway workers eating meals around the clock and booking all the sleeping rooms upstairs every night. For the next few months, Charles, Bob, and Fred poured their hearts into their new venture. They had the building repainted and hired new staff.

Then came the stock market crash and the start

of the Great Depression.

"Inside two weeks, all our railway workers were transferred to larger cities and the town began turning into a ghost town," says Charles. "Things were getting worse for us by the day, and I could see that we would soon be broke and have to close the place down."

In December, after six months of trying to succeed in Kindersley, the men closed the café and sold the restaurant's stock to the man they earlier hired to repaint the building.

"He gave us a cheque for the full amount," says Charles, who also asked the new owner to hold on to his stock of guns until Charles and the others found another town to settle. They packed up their belongings, including the store's stock of cigarettes and chocolate bars, and hopped on another freight train. They alighted at Saskatoon and went straight to the bank to cash the painter's $140 cheque. It didn't take long to learn they'd been had. The man didn't even have a bank account.

Charles, Bob, and Fred hopped yet another freight train, this time to Edmonton. It was a long and miserable ride. Winter had set in and they nearly froze to death, being without heavy coats, mitts, or caps. When the frozen trio arrived in the Alberta capital, they rented a cheap room and started to look for work. To make ends meet, they sold their stock of candy and tobacco.

But bad luck still dogged them.

There had been a robbery a few days earlier at a nearby drugstore. When the police found out that three young Saskatchewan men were selling tobacco products on the street, they quickly picked Charles and his two companions as prime suspects.

One night shortly after the robbery, Bob failed to return to the dingy hotel room. Charles phoned the police to report his brother missing and, after giving officers a description, he was told Bob had been arrested and charged with stealing goods from the drugstore.

Charles went right down to the station. When the Edmonton police phoned their counterparts in Kindersley, the latter vouched for the trio's good character and Bob was set free.

With no money left for food or a place to sleep, the trio's fortunes turned from bad to worse. They found a soup kitchen and stayed the night. The following morning, they were covered in lice. Somehow, they scraped together enough pennies to buy a can of chicken louse powder to sprinkle in their underwear.

A newspaper advertisement looking for labourers at a farm in Stoney Plain, west of Edmonton, caught their eye. However, it was the dead of winter and too cold to hop another freight train to get to there. The resourceful Charles raised $5 by pawning a gold watch he won in a poker game. It was enough for three train tickets.

When the trio arrived in Stoney Plain, they found out the farm was another 20 kilometres away. They walked all the way, only to be told by the owner's wife that her husband wasn't home and wasn't hiring anyhow. Nevertheless, the woman was kind and gave the men a meal of fresh bread, butter, and milk. They wolfed it down and then walked back to the train station, tired and beaten.

"I can remember I had a hole worn through the sole of one of my shoes," says Charles, "and every so often I had to put cardboard inside, which didn't last long."

Their cousin Fred stayed in Stoney Plain to work for free room and board at a ranch, but Charles and Bob decided it was time to go back home to Vidora. The pair returned to Edmonton, where they rode a freight train the next day to Calgary.

Their luck began to turn in Calgary. Charles knew a man who once hailed from Vidora. They were able to stay the night with him, get cleaned up, and have a good meal. The next morning, the brothers hopped the train once more, this time going as far as Lethbridge. Next day they boarded a box car on another train to Vidora. Their one-year struggle finally reached an end. The two arrived home on Christmas Day, and their anxious but grateful father was there to greet them. "Well, the big operators have come home to roost," he mused.

Charles's dad already knew what sort of trouble the boys had gotten themselves into. A stack of unpaid bills from Kindersley had piled up. He told the bill collectors his sons would return to Kindersley in the spring to settle all accounts. So, it was soon back to work — at home.

"We were quite happy that it was all over," says Charles, who remained in the Vidora area until his move in 1941 to Shaunavon.

In 1933, Charles met Grace and they married the following year. He bought a house and moved it to the family farm. In 1936, he was elected to the rural municipal council, the same year he entered the horse-buying profession. Things were looking up for Charles, but not for Vidora, still gripped by the Depression.

"It was hard times. The municipal budget was around $1000 per year," says Wilson Swihart. "Many of the people couldn't pay their taxes so they'd have a tax sale — but often there would be no takers. The town doctor became the medical health officer, and they paid him about $10 per month. It was a nickel and dime economy in Vidora."

The minutes from the village council meetings in the 1930s confirm Wilson's recollection of Vidora's tumbling fortunes. The minutes of October 5, 1933, record a desperate appeal to the provincial government for food and clothing relief. The following year, the council passed a motion to ban the use of electricity for anything except light. Those who didn't comply risked having their electricity cut off. Considering that electricity only came to Vidora in 1932, this was a hard pill to swallow.

"It came to the attention of the council that Mrs. 'Doc' Johnstone was running a radio. She was notified right away to cease and desist this activity or they would cut off her power," says Wilson. "Though radios draw very little power, I guess they thought that was still too much."

Even the newly appointed secretary-treasurer of the council, local John Rossall, felt the bite of hard times. Council voted him a salary of $10 a month, but then also voted to take half of that salary to pay off the man's tax arrears.

The last village council meeting was held in 1941. Among the body's final acts before being dissolved was the authorizing of a town official to rip up much of Vidora's wooden sidewalks and to pile all the lumber outside the town hall, beside all the community's pulled-out light poles. The end was closing in on Vidora.

There are no businesses today in Vidora. The townsite is empty and fenced off for livestock grazing. An empty cement block, once the vault for the municipal office, sits forlornly in the middle of the field. Only one residence remains, the home of Bert and Velma Richards, who run the post office for the district. Wilson is still on his farm in 2003. He is a collector of sorts, and makes special note of the former town policeman's billy club he found years ago inside in an old shop ready to be demolished.

Charles is still living Shaunavon in 2003 and pleased to talk about Vidora's pioneer days and his box car adventures. "Those early days during the Depression were disastrous for sure," he says, "but the experience has stuck with me for many years. It was one real adventure."

Senate, Saskatchewan
Sweet Music

hey were hardly rock 'n' roll stars, but for more than half a century the Senators were the biggest music sensation along the Red Coat Trail.

Led by the band's saxophone virtuoso, Paul Kalmring, and featuring Paul's wife, Margaret, on the piano, the Senators played every week — sometimes up to four times — for most of those 50-plus years. They thrilled audiences throughout southwestern Saskatchewan, northern Montana, southeastern Alberta, and even as far away as Regina. And no matter how bad or desperate things were financially or weather-wise, or how far the band had to travel by either automobile or train, they always went home after every show. After a little sleep, it was back to work farming or at their businesses in the Senate area.

"Paul ran the store in Senate, but he was very energetic," says Liz Burr, a former resident of the Senate area. "He played at our 25th wedding anniversary, and at our daughter's wedding."

From 1916 to 1983, Paul and his family were fixtures in Senate, so named after the federal body of the day when the hamlet was created in 1914. The Kalmring family moved to the area when Paul was two. His father, Paul Sr., eventually purchased a convenience store and gas station in Senate, which even in its heyday never grew past 70 citizens. In later years, Paul purchased the old Finkle Store, which also housed the post office. The Kalmring stores were the primary meeting places for locals. There they swapped stories and, when power lines were installed around Senate in 1957, Paul brought the town's first television to the Finkle Store.

"The playoff baseball and hockey games drew a big crowd of television watchers," says Margaret. "When a game went into overtime, I usually had extra meals to deliver as no one wanted to go home until the game ended."

Colourful characters frequently dropped by the

stores — locals, as well as those out-of-towners looking to start a new life. One of the latter was Hugh McKay, a street car operator from San Francisco, who fled to Senate after he thought he had beaten a man to death in his house.

"Hugh went to his lawyer and was advised to entrust the lawyer with his money and property and to leave the country," recalls Paul. "He came to Canada and got himself a homestead."

When Hugh arrived in Senate, he became the talk of the town, not because of all the stories and rumours of what he might have done, but because of the way he shouted and talked. Folks thought he was crazy. One night he sawed off the foot of his bed thinking spirits were sitting there. Neighbours often heard him screaming at his fanning mill and pounding it with a wrench.

Years later, Hugh went back to San Francisco to face his demons. He discovered his lawyer had taken all his money and property. His wife had vanished as well. However, the biggest surprise was finding out that the man he thought he killed was very much alive. Hugh returned to Senate and sold his farm. He then headed to Yellowknife, never to be seen again.

While Hugh McKay was running away from his nightmare, others were coming to Senate to live out their hopes and dreams. More often than not, those hopes and dreams were shattered at first sight. The land was bleak, desolate, and dry. Grasshoppers and marauding rabbits had feeding frenzies on whatever crops managed to poke out from the parched soil.

Charlotte Reynolds arrived in Senate in 1931 after meeting her husband, Bert, in her native England. Bert had already been to Canada with two older brothers, working for the Canadian Pacific Railway and securing a homestead northwest of the hamlet. When he met Charlotte, he sung the praises of the faraway land in Canada, with its beautiful wide open prairies and property given away for free by the government to entice immigrants to come.

"It took me over a month to get my folks' consent," says Charlotte, of her marriage and subsequent plans to move to Canada with Bert. "I had to plead for it. I really wanted to go on this big adventure."

However, it was the beginning of the "dirty '30s." There were no crops, no rain, no money. The pink-cloud of marital bliss gave way to the harsh reality that soon hit Charlotte like a freight train.

After a wondrous one-week journey by ocean liner to Canada, the young couple travelled another week by train across eastern Canada to the prairies.

"When we finally arrived in Senate, I thought I would surely die. What a place!" says Charlotte. "There was a crowd to meet us. Everyone from around knew Bert was bringing an English bride. I'm sure they must have laughed at me in my English clothes, bare legs and bobby socks — and it was cold."

There was more in store for Charlotte — much more. Bert's brothers drove the honeymooners to the bride's new Canadian residence in a beat-up jalopy. During the entire bumpy journey, the startled and horrified young woman tried to figure out how the driver could follow such a poorly defined road.

"All there was then were two deep ruts," says Charlotte. "And the residence? What a place: a kitchen, small bedroom, and lean-to for the brothers. I didn't know I would be living for three years with three men. I cried a lot and wanted to go back home."

But Charlotte stayed and grew not only to accept her new country, but to enjoy her spartan surroundings. Charlotte and Bert went on to live long happy lives, raising seven children along the way. They stayed in the Senate area until 1960, when they moved to Consul.

"I did everything so wrong at first, and I got laughed at," says Charlotte, who in 2003 is enjoying her retirement years in Maple Creek. "I had an inferiority complex, but I got over it. I came to love Canada. Everyone is on the same level. There is no class distinction here."

At about the same time as Charlotte's arrival in Senate, Paul began clerking in the hamlet's family store. He bought a Model-T car because his duties included delivering shipments of coal and gas to customers and meeting the train on Tuesdays and Fridays to pick up groceries.

When he had time during his bachelor days, Paul took the train to Govenlock for dances. Govenlock was an especially popular destination for young men during the prohibition years — a place where export liquor stores had set up shop and where police chased rum-runners heading south to the American border.

"The train conductor never charged us," says Paul. "The men would go to play poker, drink all night, and come back home on the train the next day."

Because there was so little to do — or money to spend — the dances, with all their loud and brash music, took on a special meaning for Paul. He wanted to become a musician and so worked to save enough money to buy a clarinet. Playing the instrument became his passion, wherever he was. "When the store was empty, I would practice — but I didn't want to chase anybody away," chuckles Paul.

After a year with his new instrument, Paul was forced to make a change after injuring his index finger while tightening lids on canned meat at the store. In

1933, Paul Sr. went to Havre, Montana, and picked up a trumpet for his son, explaining to the younger Kalmring that he'd "always have enough fingers" for his new instrument.

Two years later though, Paul switched again, this time to the saxophone. It was to become his signature instrument for the next half century.

By 1935, Paul felt he had practised enough at the family store. He wanted to start a dance band. By then he'd also met Margaret, who was skilled at pounding out the day's most popular dance tunes on the piano. Joining them was drummer Nick Schafer, who had learned the art of music-making from his father, a band player in the Russian army.

"Margaret, Paul, and I were the 'Old Faithfuls' of the Senators," says Nick. "Many times we played our music for free, at wedding dances and charitable affairs. I missed out on the dancing, but it gave me a chance from my place on the platform to survey all the romancing going on the dance floor, and to size up the good-looking girls, especially the new teachers."

As it turned out, Nick did meet his future wife, Florence, that way and married her in 1947, with the wedding dance — hosted by the Senators — held in Senate.

Many other locals contributed to the orchestra over the years, including guitarist Jack Howe (who later taught Paul how to read music), Bill Finkle, Jimmie Munro, Kurt Browatzke, Les Marlin, and Art Jones. Paul's daughter Irene, who also played sax, joined the band too.

For half a century — except during the war years when Paul served in the Canadian army — not one week went by when the Senators weren't playing somewhere. Paul always made sure to close his store's door by 6 p.m. to give him and the band time to get to a show. They travelled along the Red Coat Trail to Govenlock, Vidora, Consort, Robsart, Eastend, and Shaunavon, northeast to Regina, and south to Climax and Havre, Montana. They also played regularly in Alberta, hitting the dusty trails to Manyberries and Orion.

As the decades rolled by, age didn't prevent the Senators' "barnstorming" tours, even if the fate of many pioneer towns in southwestern Saskatchewan was becoming grim. By the 1970s, several towns along the Red Coat Trail were becoming ghost towns or had vanished altogether. Senate was headed the same way. Paul Kalmring stayed on, his hopes for the future propelled by his music. In 1980, he sold the store and retired to his farm three kilometres north of Senate, but the music-making continued. Although most of the other contributors to the Senators had moved or retired to other locales, Paul and Margaret carried on playing their saxophone and piano for senior citizens, community programs, concerts, and churches.

In 1983, the new store owner in Senate closed shop. That signaled the end of the hamlet. In 1994, with the railway and elevators also gone, rural municipality officials brought in the bulldozers and levelled Senate's remaining dilapidated buildings. Part of the debris was dumped into a nearby landfill.

"It died a bad death," Paul says sadly.

Every once in a while, though, he returns to the bluff alongside the Red Coat Trail where his store once stood. It's usually silent there, except for the cars passing by on the highway. Still, if the wind blows just right, memories of the sweet music from days long past can be heard, a ghostly reminder of a time when the Senators played their magic throughout the land.

Govenlock, Saskatchewan
No-Guff Gaff

I t was October 16, 1917. "Dad" Gaff was in a boisterous mood. He was well on his way to getting good and drunk on an old bottle of Scotch, his favourite drink. His cowboy cronies, who were hooting and hollering with each of Dad's grand old stories, were not letting up either. If anything, they were getting more fired up to party and raise hell raise all the way to sunrise. This was, after all, Cypress Hills country and the land of Govenlock, Saskatchewan — the land where booze and foot-stomping wild living was an accepted way of life.

The men had had an exhausting day. It had begun

at the crack of dawn the previous morning when they left a rip-roaring stampede adventure in Chinook, Montana, travelling home on horseback. The ride to Dad's ranch at Battle Creek, located about 23 kilometres north of Govenlock, was long. Now it was time to unwind.

At the age of 67, Dad (named James Aaron at birth) was much older than some of his friends. And while he was known by everybody in Govenlock and throughout the Cypress Hills as Dad, he still had a streak of youthful exuberance, a trait he never surrendered even after his buffalo-hunting days on the American plains with "Buffalo Bill" Cody and Wild Bill Hickock. He may have been getting a bit long in the tooth, but he could still party and regale anyone who would listen with tales of buffalo hunting and Wild West living.

Eventually his pals needed shut-eye, and Dad gathered them up and took them into town to the Govenlock Hotel, a two-storey, 10-bedroom joint built four years earlier by John Lindner. When they arrived, Dad was told there were no rooms left for either him or his buddies. He was not going to sit quietly over this piece of information.

He and the troupe of cowboys banged on the tables and counters in the hotel's dining room. Dad turned to Lindner and let him know, with his most colourful cowboy language and gestures, how he felt about a hotel that wouldn't take care of his swaggering pals.

Lindner sternly told him the cost to stay would be in four figures. "It's a darned sight more than you can put up, Gaff," he huffed.

Dad was not about to be bested in front of his pals.

"Is that so?" he bellowed. "Well, I'll buy the whole place! What do you want for it?"

Lindner sneered, but shot back, "Forty-five hundred dollars."

Without missing a beat, Dad pulled out his pocket book and wrote Lindner a cheque, buying the hotel on the spot. His rowdy friends had their rooms for the night and another Dad Gaff legend was born.

For many years after that, Dad held court at the Govenlock Hotel. In 1917, Govenlock was still an infant frontier community in southwestern Saskatchewan, but it was already earning a reputation as a spot where liquor flowed freely and cowboys were welcome to party. If Dad was looking for the perfect place away from his family at Battle Creek ranch, a place to settle down and jaw, there was no better locale than the Govenlock Hotel.

Four years earlier, before the arrival of the railway, Moose Jaw businessman William Govenlock negotiated a land sale agreement with the Canadian Pacific Railway to build a townsite. When the rail line was extended to

Govenlock in 1914, it was a guarantee to settlers that a steady flow of supplies would reach the new town and its growing number of businesses — most notably the four export liquor warehouses.

Although Saskatchewan was considered a "dry" province at the time, provincial laws were modified to allow the production and export of liquor and beer. So, when the state government in Montana introduced prohibition in 1919, businessmen in Govenlock could not believe their good luck. They were already doing a booming business in the liquor trade, but Montana's new law ensured huge fortunes. The international whiskey trade was on, and out came a legion of rum-runners, bootleggers, and outlaws who shuttled back and forth from Havre, Montana. Always, they were either watched or chased by Mounties or Saskatchewan Provincial Police.

Businessmen in Govenlock didn't mind the influx of seedy characters. In fact, they seized the opportunity to get rich quickly. The Govenlock family led the way by converting its warehouse into a liquor export operation. The Bronfman brothers of Yorkton, Saskatchewan, opened up another, as did Lethbridge's Archie McCorvic and Joe Bonfadini.

"It was a wide open run for us here," says Tom Buchanan, whose father Howard was employed in the

Govenlock prohibition booze trade. "My dad used to talk about the times he would be unloading the liquor off the trains, which would be coming in at all hours. Everything came in bags at that time, even the beer."

"Some of the liquor sold really well and some didn't," Tom continues. "One of my dad's jobs was taking all the liquor that didn't sell and pouring it into metal or copper tubs. This was then put into the bottles that sold the best and out it went again. People didn't know any better."

Meanwhile, rum-runners had their own schedule to meet, and the townspeople witnessed the daily ritual of open cloth touring cars — with licence plates from all over the U.S. — pulling into Govenlock every afternoon. The drivers, who made their border crossings at night, first headed over to the Grant Brothers' pool hall, where high-stakes poker action was hot. They were usually joined by eager local businessmen. If they were hungry, there was always home-cooked country food in the dining room at the Govenlock Hotel, along with the non-stop chatter from Dad Gaff.

When the sun went down, it was time for work. One by one, the drivers backed into the warehouses to load up their Fords, Packards, Hudsons, Studebakers, and Coles. Most of the vehicles were equipped with special auxiliary leaf springs to accommodate the extra weight.

Quarts of the coveted 12 percent Canadian beer were first wrapped tightly in straw and then packaged in three sacks, each of them holding 24 bottles. Next, the sacks were stuffed in a barrel, which wholesaled for $20 and sold for $144 in the United States. Meanwhile, a 12-bottle case of liquor wholesaled for between $32 and $50, and sold double that back home.

Drivers, often hauling loads of 14 barrels of beer and five cases of whiskey south of the border, saw their profits soar. They could make as much as $2500 in a run. With that much money at stake, drivers were forced to run the gauntlet of highjackers and outlaws on their way back to Havre. Howard Buchanan was fond of telling locals about one Green Essex coupe that had a built-in bullet-proof boiler plate behind the seat.

"One of the leading haulers was Tex Hunter out of Great Falls, Montana," recalled Howard years later. "His wife was also a driver. She was eventually mistakenly shot by her husband."

With desperate men constantly running rum back and forth from Govenlock to the border, encounters between locals and outlaws were common. Knowing that these men were armed and more often than not running from the law with frayed nerves, residents did their best to avoid trouble.

Many times, the booty never made it to the border.

One rum-runner was shot and killed making a dash to the line. And many times the booze was stolen off the back of trucks or drays while being unloaded from the trains.

One evening in 1922, Howard was working in the countryside between Govenlock and the border when he noticed a southbound car stop briefly by the roadside. On his way home, he rode his horse to where the vehicle had parked. He followed the tire tracks to a clump of sage brush and found two sacks of beer. Tying these to his horse, he cheerfully walked the eight kilometres home. In town, he sold the beer and found a poker game, promptly losing all the money he'd just come into.

Thirty years later, when Howard shared this story with former Govenlock Hotel owner John Lindner, John said to him, "Howard if you'd gone a few more rods, you'd have found the whiskey too."

The same year that Howard found his beer stash in the sagebrush, Govenlock's hell-raising days came to an end. The Saskatchewan government introduced legislation to restrict the liquor export houses to cities of 10,000 citizens or more.

When Govenlock's decline began in 1922, Dad Gaff was firmly settled in at his hotel. He was 72 years old and somewhat retired.

It had been a long trail ride for Dad that led him to southwestern Saskatchewan. He was born in Noble County, Indiana, in 1850. One Gaff relative traced the family roots back to a pre-Civil War plantation owner in the south who had had 3500 slaves but later fought against slavery in the war. It's known that Dad went west to Kansas at the age of 18. It was on the Kansas plains where he first started buffalo hunting. These were the days when buffalo still roamed the prairies in the millions and when plainsmen played the Wild West part to the letter, wearing long hair and bushy beards.

Out on the plains, Dad carried his old "Mary Ann" — his 12-pound Sharps rifle. He became friends and hunting partners with American legends William "Buffalo Bill" Cody and "Wild Bill" Hickock. He also had run-ins with angry Natives and encounters with outlaws, including Billy the Kid.

He began his buffalo-hunting days in the 1870s. He used a technique that would receive widespread public condemnation in later years and was banned in the 20th century. He went out onto the plains and killed buffalo for their tongues alone. On a typical outing, Dad would shoot six to eight animals, cut out their tongues, strap them onto his saddle, and later sell them for 50 cents each. The tongues, considered a delicacy in eastern states, were pickled and shipped to the finest shops and restaurants.

In later years, Dad formed a buffalo-hide hunter's camp, which included up to six skinners and haulers. When the herds were plentiful, good incomes were guaranteed. With his Sharps rifle, Dad usually felled a buffalo in two shots. On one notable day, Dad shot and killed 80 buffaloes. In the camp's best seasons, his crew killed more than 5200 animals, collecting between $1 and $4 for each hide.

Along the buffalo-hunting trails, there was always adventure. During one expedition on August 31, 1871, Dad and hunting partner John Campbell were working a large herd along the dried-up creek channels in Kansas' Sheridan County. Dad, already a veteran hunter at the age of 21, was more skilled than his partner, who was eagerly trying to prove himself as a proficient marksman. From a distance of more than a kilometre and a half away, they sighted a lone buffalo sleeping far from the main herd. The pair picked a spot on a creek bank and waited to see if the main herd came their way. They hesitated to shoot the single bull lest the noise cause a stampede.

"I wish I had him by the horns, so I could hold him while you cut his throat," John said to Dad, itching to show his toughness. "I think I could catch him while he was asleep."

Dad was impressed with the rookie's enthusiasm,

but he also wanted to have a little fun. He agreed to go along with the plan. As Dad loaded his old Mary Ann, John crept towards the sleeping buffalo. Dad fired a single shot and the bull went down. John grabbed the animal's horns, but as quick as the injured beast went down, it was just as fast getting back onto its feet. Dad's moment of fun went into overdrive.

The buffalo bolted, with John gripping the horns for dear life. After about two minutes, with the adventure becoming increasingly dangerous, John screamed at Dad, "Jim, shoot, damn it! Shoot!"

As Dad aimed his Mary Ann for the final kill, he knew his shot had to be perfect. The blast knocked down the bull. Clearly shaken, John swore at Dad for not firing sooner. That was the end of John's buffalo hunting for the day. Dad, meanwhile, went on to shoot 14 more, the highest number he ever recorded in a single stand.

Dad continued to buffalo hunt until 1877, when he decided to settle down in Kansas to farm. He soon tired of farming and headed to Nebraska to raise cattle. By 1894, however, Nebraska was filling up with settlers, and horse thieves were making their mark in the state. Dad opted to sell off his cattle and land and take his family by covered wagon to Utah, and then, shortly after, to Canada. He was determined to make his fortune as a cattle rancher.

Once in Canada, Dad and his family settled on Battle Creek. He purchased a large stock of cattle and later became known as the "Great Cattle Baron" of the Cypress Hills.

By 1913, Dad was keenly aware that the days of the open ranges were coming to an end. He and his family hosted a huge party to celebrate the end of that glorious pioneer era. It was what Dad and his clan called the "Last Big Old-Timer's Dance." Cowboys from both sides of the border joined residents from every part of the Battle Creek region at the party. The Gaffs were an immensely popular family, renowned region-wide for helping out new settlers by donating horses to start them farming.

"As you arrived at the ranch in the evening, the Gaffs' son-in-law, John Boon, offered you a big swig of rum from a one-gallon crock," wrote George Shepherd for the *Saskatoon Star Phoenix*. The reporter's family lived seven kilometres from the Gaff clan. "Your horses were stabled or tied to the corral rails and you made your way to the house. It was all lit up and the din inside was terrific.

"A local Métis named Whitford was sawing away on a violin as though he would saw it in two, sweat streaming down his face and beating time with his moccasined foot," continued Shepherd. "Added to this were the shouts of the dance callers. The house was set up for square dancing, but if you preferred round dancing you took your girl outside in the cool night air where the Lane Brothers played their violins for the quieter round dances."

The dance may have marked the end of an era, but four years later Dad started a new one by buying the Govenlock Hotel. He brought along his daughter Alla to live with him and she minded the hotel business while Dad relaxed with the patrons. He still held an interest in the Cypress Hills ranch and went there from time to time to visit family. However, most of his retirement days were spent back at the hotel with his beloved bottle of Scotch, swapping stories with his favourite cowboy cronies and playing pinochle.

"I still have the old pinochle deck and chips they used years and years ago. He was a great player," recalls grandson Nile Gaff in 2003. "Dad used to say he had one Scotch in the morning, one at noon, and one at night.

Dad died on January 28, 1941, shortly after celebrating his 90th birthday. Alla died several months later in 1941. She had married Andy McRae in 1933 and they had purchased the hotel from Dad. Andy later remarried and continued to run the hotel. When he passed away in 1974, the hotel was once again purchased by the Gaff family. By that time, though, Govenlock had become a ghost town and the hotel was falling apart. It joined several other derelict buildings in the frontier town.

"My brother Leo bought the hotel with two of his neighbours," says Nile, "but the rural municipality wanted to charge them taxes going back years. Leo argued they hadn't owned it in the days when taxes weren't paid, but it was to no avail."

All the furnishings and fixtures, including doors and windows, were eventually auctioned off. A few hotel chairs still remain with Gaff family members today.

In 1988, the hotel caught fire while being bulldozed. Three years later, the rural municipality hired a contractor to demolish Govenlock's other remaining derelict buildings, including the old general store, the garage, and John Lindner's former home. It was a sad and final end for the once lively frontier town.

Today, only the community hall (built in 1948) and a commemorative plaque mark the location of the former town.

"Dad was certainly one of a kind — a true pioneer spirit who touched many people's lives," says Nile. "There will never be another like him."

Epilogue
Ongoing Journeys

This is not the final chapter on the pioneer communities and people of the Red Coat Trail. There are many more stories to tell, and many more yet to come.

It has been five years since Don Sucha went to Wood Mountain, and he is far from finished learning about Constable Daniel "Peach" Davis. Despite the doubts of some RCMP historians, Don is satisfied that Peach did single-handedly escort well over 200 Assiniboine more than 250 kilometres to the reserves near Battleford.

During his extensive research, he has located a

19th-century *Saskatchewan Herald* newspaper clipping with an article headlined "Back to the Grub Pile." For Don, it confirmed Peach's story, as passed down to family members over the years.

"During the past week, several hundred of the Indians who have been spending their time at the south arrived here," noted the article. "They were furnished with provisions at Cypress to bring them a part of the way across the plains, and another lot was dispatched from this side to meet them. Constable Davis took charge of the first lot of provisions and had general management of the pilgrims."

The article went on to describe the tragic killing of a member of Peach's Assiniboine group by the Blackfoot during the journey. Previous historical accounts reported bitter conflicts between the two First Nations bands. The *Herald* piece described the incident in detail.

"Shortly before these people [Assiniboine] left Fort Walsh, a large body of Blackfoot visited that place and held a war dance," said the article, adding that the visitors had also stolen horses during the night. "In the course of the night they got hold of [an Assiniboine] and killed him. When found in the morning he was pierced with about 50 bullets. This was good evidence that he was dead and showed the Blackfoot had a grand jubilee over the occurrence."

Don's research has not confirmed whether Peach's remarkable journey began at the U.S. border. He is still chipping away, hoping some day to stumble upon a piece of information that will confirm the truth.

Meanwhile, another Peach mystery has unfolded as a result of Don's ongoing investigation.

When Don returned from his family trip to Wood Mountain, he sent a request to the National Archives in Ottawa for Peach's service record with the North West Mounted Police. When it arrived, he discovered a sad and unsettling letter in the file written to the RCMP by a Calgary man in 1960. The man said his wife had been going through some old trunks in their house and came across an old military medal that she had had since she was a child. It was a medal of service from the 1885 North West Rebellion.

"Any information you would give us about this medal, such as the ribbon colours, the reason for awarding it, and if possible a bit of history about the man to whom it was awarded would be greatly appreciated," wrote the man. He went on to say that while the medal was somewhat tarnished, there was a clear inscription that said "North West 1885 Canada," encircled by a maple leaf wreath. Another inscription on the edge of the medal said "581 Constable Davis."

Where did his great grand-uncle's medal end up,

Don wants to know. "From the description, it doesn't sound like the medal is in very good condition or would be of any great value to a collector," says Don. "But it would be of emotional value to me, as well as historical, as it is a final punctuation mark to the whole story."

There were 5650 North West medals issued, but only 920 given to the North West Mounted Police. The latter had names inscribed; the others didn't.

Don later called the funeral home that handled Peach's arrangements after his death in 1937. He was told that, in keeping with Peach's instructions, his medal had been removed and was to have been presented to his wife before burial. The RCMP responded to the Calgarian man's 1960 letter only by confirming that Peach had served at the North West Rebellion and was finally discharged at Fort Macleod in 1886.

"There have been no further developments on the issue," says Don. "I have tried to check all that I see in museums but have had no luck so far. I have acquaintances who collect medals and I have them keeping an eye open for me. Because the medal was in such bad condition as described in the letter, I fear that it's simply gone. But stranger things have happened in my quest for Peach Davis, so you never know."

My quest also continues. I was last on the Red Coat Trail in September 2002. My trip took me to Scotsguard,

Bateman, Ravenscrag, Dollard, Robsart, and Govenlock. With each passing year, these communities are fading a little more and becoming breeding grounds for fast-tumbling Russian thistles.

There remains a heartbeat in some Red Coat Trail towns, like Manyberries and Etzikom. A few residents balk at the notion their communities are ghost towns, insisting there is still life and a future ahead. Although populations in both communities have dropped below 50, there is a glimmer of hope that in another 50 years there will be more stories to tell. But for me, the right time is now. Otherwise, as Nemiskam's Derek McNaney said, the living history of our heritage will be lost.

I think of Senate's Paul Kalmring playing saxophone on the rise where his town once stood above the Red Coat Trail. If we talk to Paul, and understand why he played, then his sweet music will never fade. It will be ours forever.

Bibliography

Anderson, Frank W. *The Dynamic Crow's Nest*. Calgary, AB: Frontier Publishing Ltd., 1969.

Anderson, Frank W. *Outlaws of Manitoba*. Calgary, AB: Frontier Publishing Ltd., 1971.

Anderson, Frank W. *The Rum Runners*. Edmonton, AB: Lone Pine Publishing, 1991.

Basque, Garnet (ed.). *Frontier Days in Alberta*. Langley, BC: Sunfire Publications Ltd., 1992.

Chatenay, Henri. *The Country Doctors*. Red Deer, AB: Mattrix Press, 1980.

Knuckle, Robert. *In the Line of Duty: The Honour Roll of the RCMP Since 1873*. Burnstown, ON: General Store Publishing, 1994.

MacEwan, Grant. *Sitting Bull: The Years in Canada*. Edmonton, AB: Hurtig Publishers, 1973.

Bibliography

Moore, Frank. *Saskatchewan Ghost Towns*. Regina, SK: Associated Printers, 1982.

Primrose, Tom. *The Cypress Hills*. Calgary, AB: Frontier Publishing Ltd., 1969.

Russell, E.T. *What's in a Name: The Story Behind Saskatchewan Place Names*. Markham, ON: Fifth House Ltd., 1997.

Wilson, Gary A. *Honky Tonk Town: Havre's Bootlegging Days*. Havre, MT: High-Line Books, 1985.

Photograph Credits

All photographs by Johnny Bachusky except page 48 which is reproduced courtesy of the Etzikom Museum of Southeast Alberta.

Acknowledgments

The following local community history books provided me with valuable sources of information for this book:*Shortgrass Country* published by Foremost Historical Society; *Our Side of the Hills* by Reno History Book Association; *From Sage to Timber* by the Merry Battlers Ladies Club; *Between and Beyond the Benches* by Ravenscrag History Book Committee; and *Next Year Country* by Notukeu History Book Club.

As well, past editions of regional newspapers proved invaluable for my research, notably Regina's *The Leader-Post* (March 18 and 19, 1940) for the prologue, *The Medicine Hat News* (December 1916) for the chapter on Manyberries, and *The Western Producer* (December 1, 1960) for the Govenlock chapter.

I also wish to extend my deep appreciation and gratitude to the many people who contributed their time and stories for this book. Because of the number of people, it is impossible for me to list everyone. However, I must extend a special thanks to Vivian Stuber, president of the Manyberries Historical Association, for her help with both the Manyberries and Orion chapters.

Acknowledgments

I also thank Calgary's Don Sucha. Don and I are kindred spirits of sorts. His expertise is in the study of cemeteries. His commitment to and extraordinary help with this book are greatly appreciated. Finally, I would like to thank my late friend Geoff Payne, who I knew well in the 1990s while I worked at the Kerby Centre. After our trip to Highway 61, Geoff mentioned that some day it might be a good idea to write a book. It's done Geoff, and thank you.

As well, I'd like to offer a special thank-you to Toronto web designers Susan Foster and Jeri Danyleyko, co-founders of www.ghosttownpix.com, for the support they've given me on this project and my ongoing ghost town journeys.

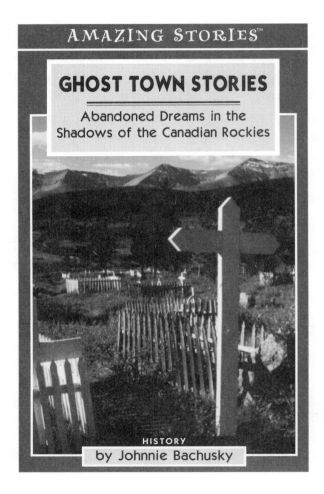

AMAZING STORIES™

GHOST TOWN STORIES

Abandoned Dreams in the
Shadows of the Canadian Rockies

HISTORY
by Johnnie Bachusky

Ghost Town Stories: Canadian Rockies
ISBN 1-55153-993-4

About the Author

Johnnie Bachusky has been an Alberta journalist since 1984. Over the past six and half years, he has toured hundreds of ghost towns across Western Canada and written dozens of ghost town articles and heritage-related pieces for newspapers and magazines in Canada. His heritage photography has been featured in national and international publications. He has consulted for television documentaries. As well, he is co-creator of two acclaimed ghost town web sites about Alberta and Saskatchewan. He is currently working on a web site about ghost towns of British Columbia and another on historic wooden grain elevators. He lives with his wife, Darlis, and daughter, Darlana, in Red Deer, Alberta. This is the author's second book.

OTHER AMAZING STORIES

These titles are available wherever you buy books. If you have trouble finding the book you want, call the Altitude order desk at 1-800-957-6888, e-mail your request to: orderdesk@altitudepublishing.com or visit our Web site at www.amazingstories.ca

All titles retail for $9.95 Cdn or $7.95 US. (Prices subject to change.)

New AMAZING STORIES titles are published every month. If you would like more information, e-mail your name and mailing address to: amazingstories@altitudepublishing.com.